FOR ORGANS, PIANOS & ELECTRONIC KEYBOARDS
E-Z Play Today 157
Easy Favorites

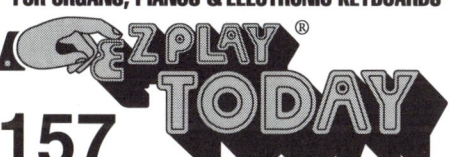

CONTENTS

Andantino	2
Aura Lee	5
Beautiful Brown Eyes	35
Camptown Races	3
Carnival Of Venice	20
Dixie	22
Down In The Valley	36
Greensleeves	6
La Spagnola	26
Lavender's Blue	16
Little Brown Jug	39
Londonderry Air	12
Long, Long Ago	8
Man On The Flying Trapeze, The	43
Maori Farewell Song	28
Marianne	46
Melody Of Love	38
Michael, Row The Boat Ashore	18
My Wild Irish Rose	14
Santa Lucia	30
Skater's Waltz, The	42
Swanee River	32
Tales From The Vienna Woods	10
Theme From "The New World" Symphony	25
When The Saints Go Marching In	34
Registration Guide	47

ISBN 0-7935-4423-8

7777 W. BLUEMOUND RD. P.O. BOX 13819 MILWAUKEE, WI 53213

E-Z PLAY ® TODAY Music Notation © 1975 HAL LEONARD CORPORATION
Copyright © 1972, 1984, 1995 by HAL LEONARD CORPORATION
International Copyright Secured   All Rights Reserved

For all works contained herein:
Unauthorized copying, arranging, adapting, recording or public performance is an infringement of copyright.
Infringers are liable under the law.

E-Z PLAY and EASY ELECTRONIC KEYBOARD MUSIC are registered trademarks of HAL LEONARD CORPORATION.

ANDANTINO

Registration 2
Rhythm: Fox Trot or Swing

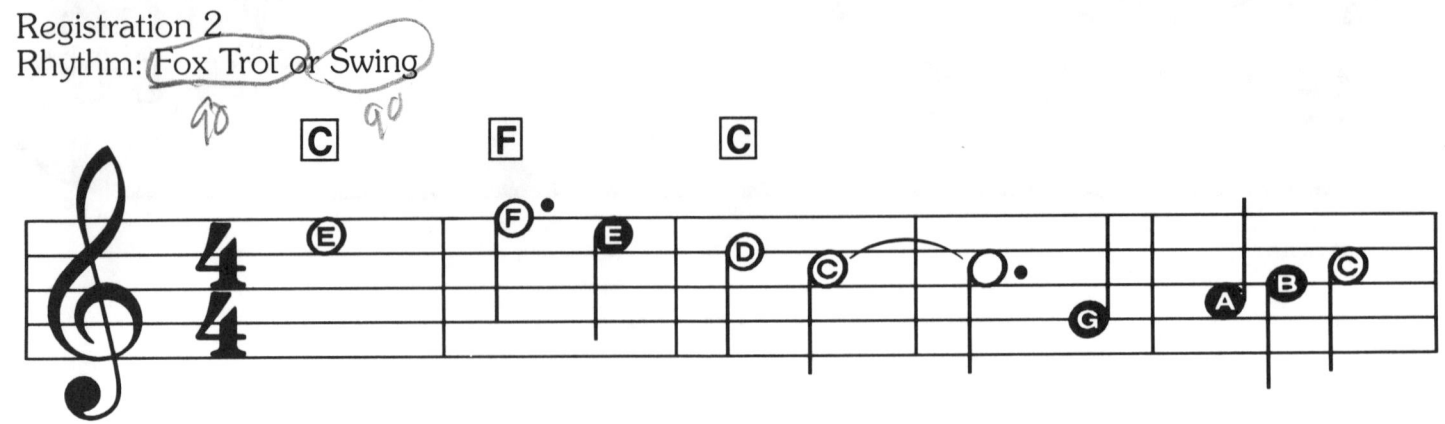

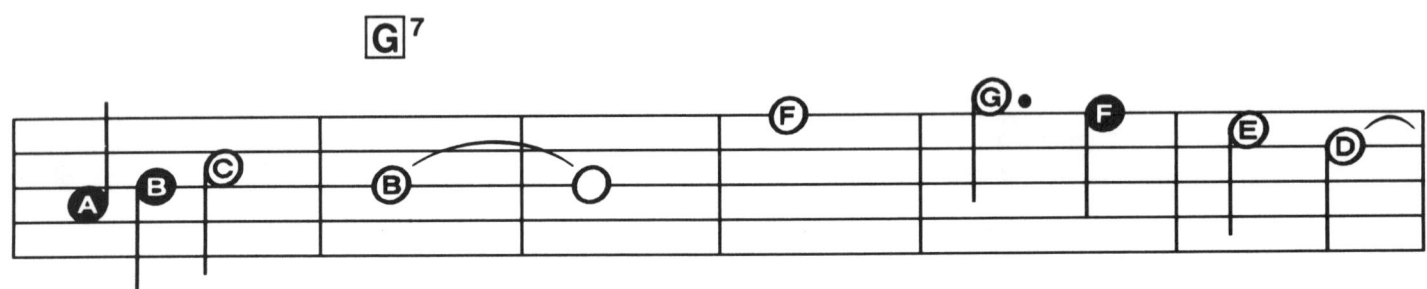

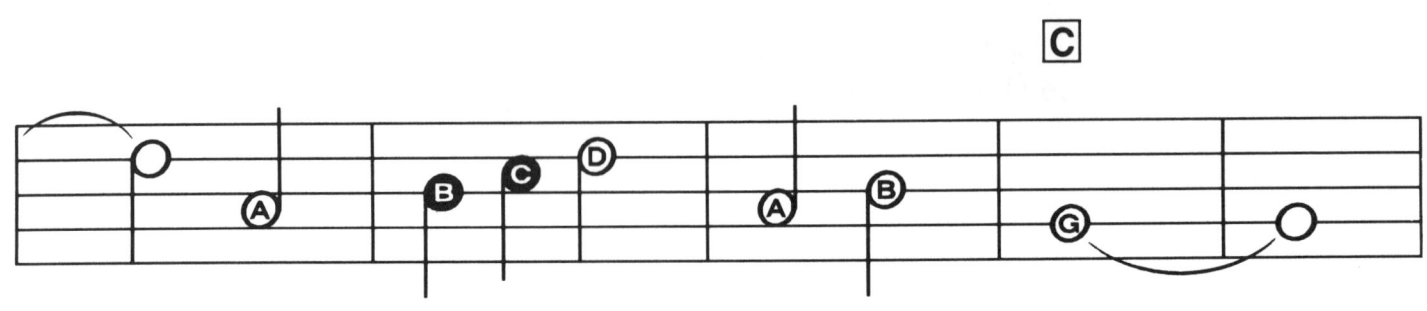

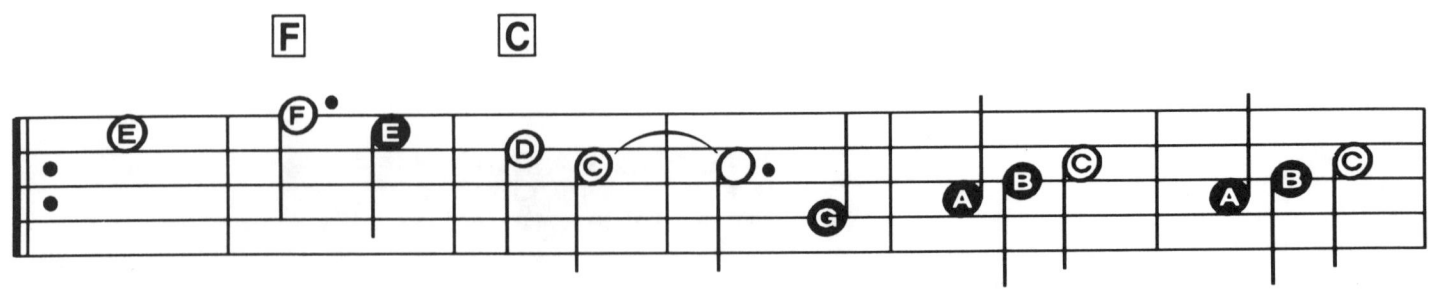

Copyright © 1972 HAL LEONARD CORPORATION
International Copyright Secured   All Rights Reserved

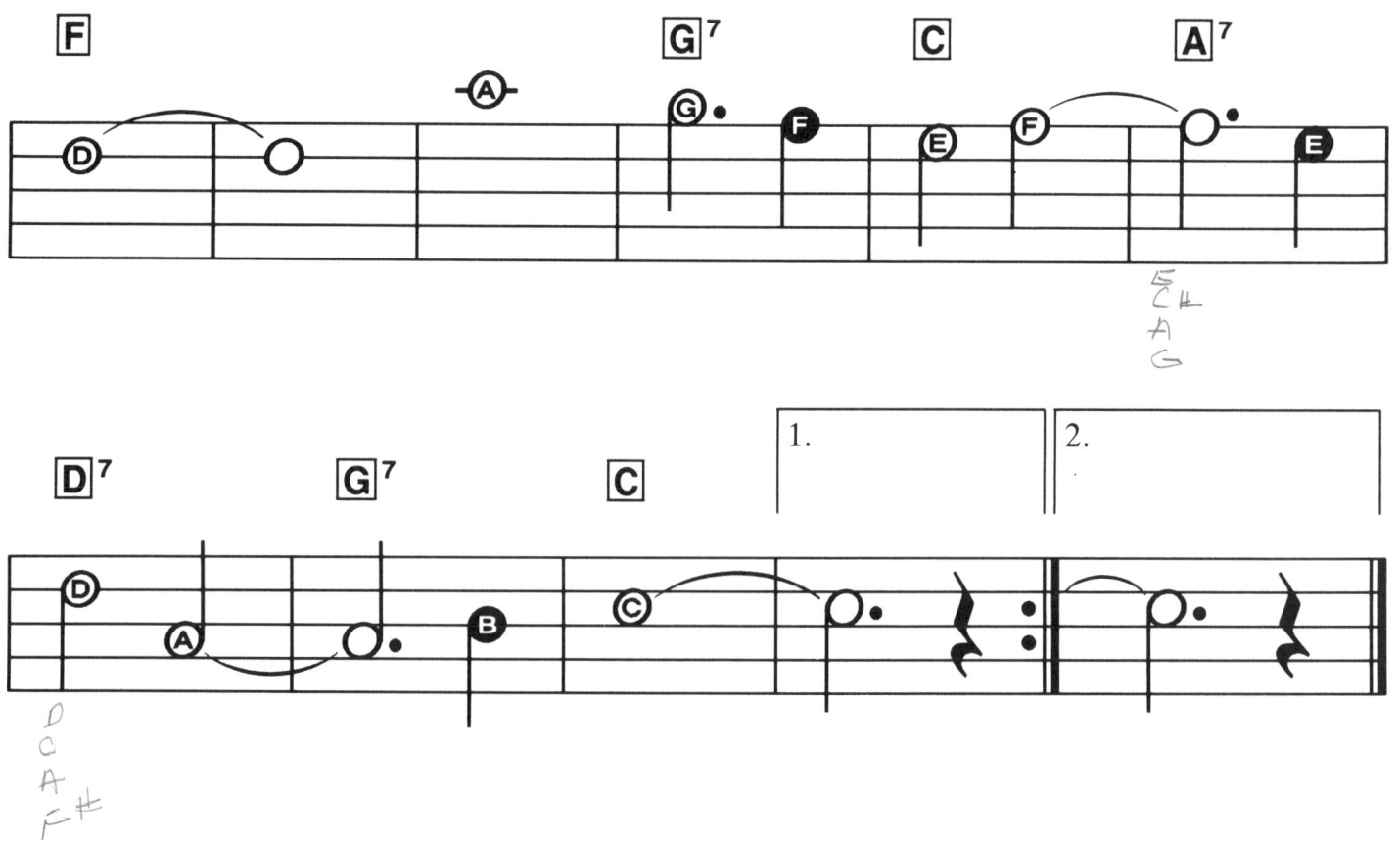

CAMPTOWN RACES

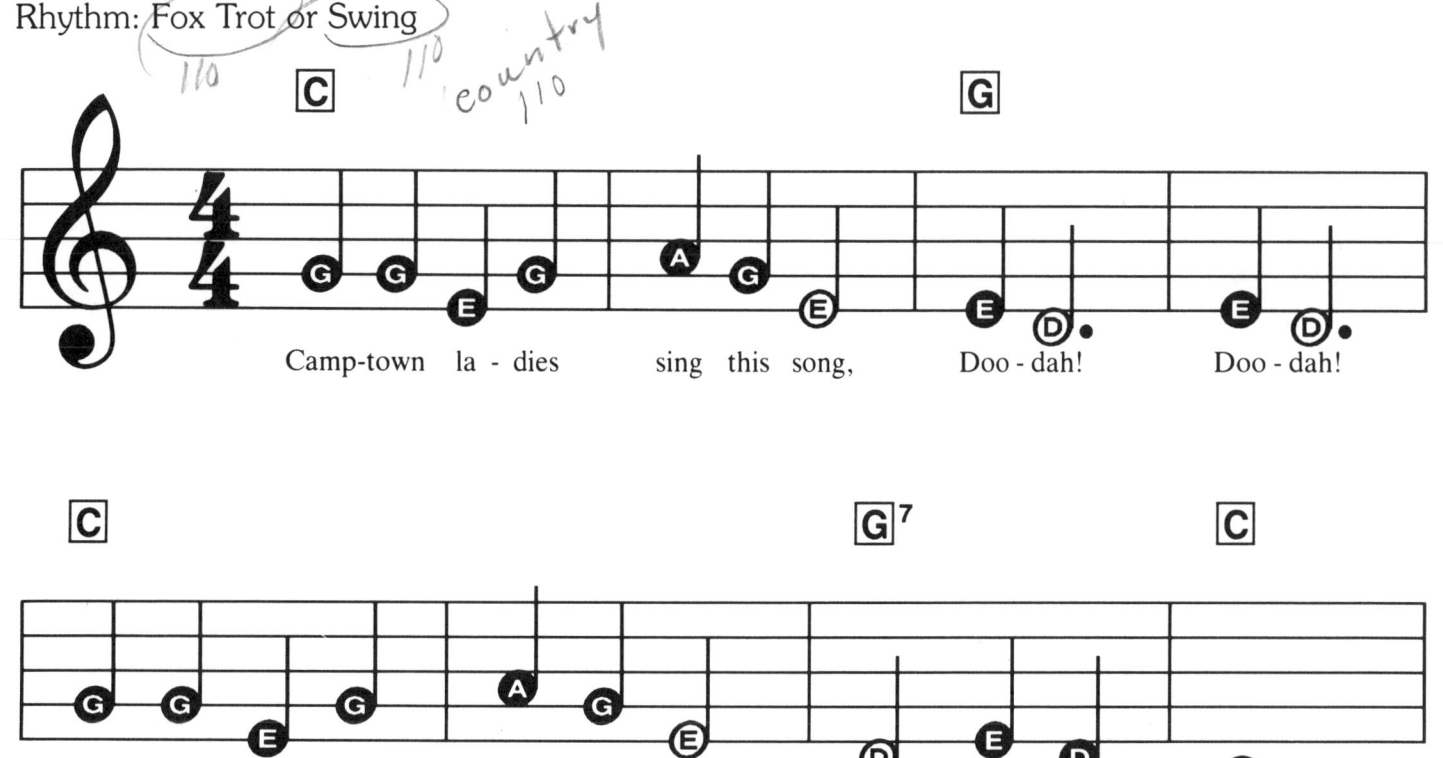

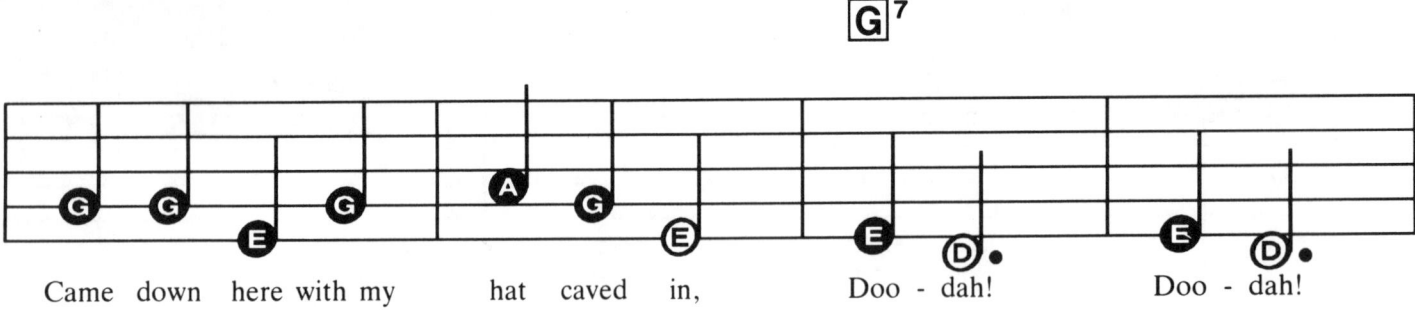
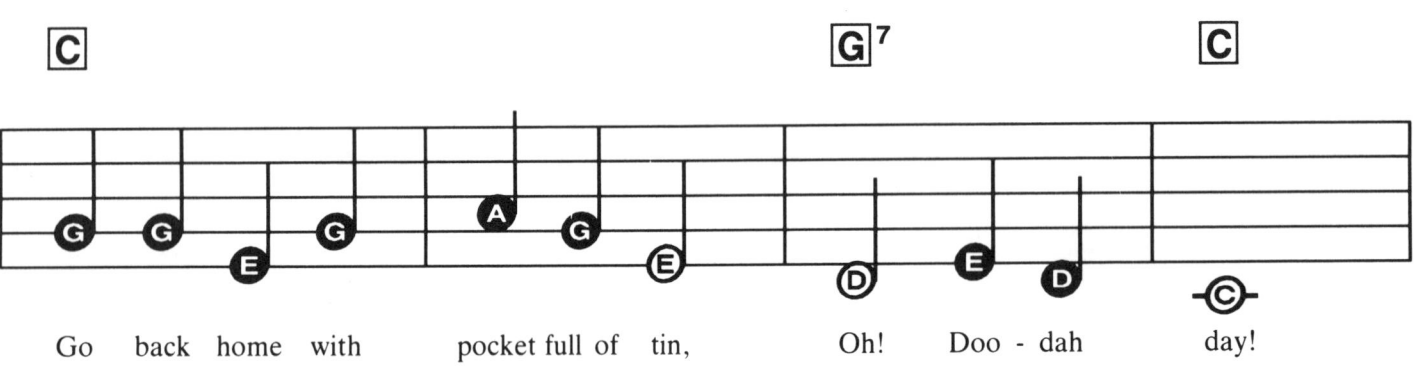
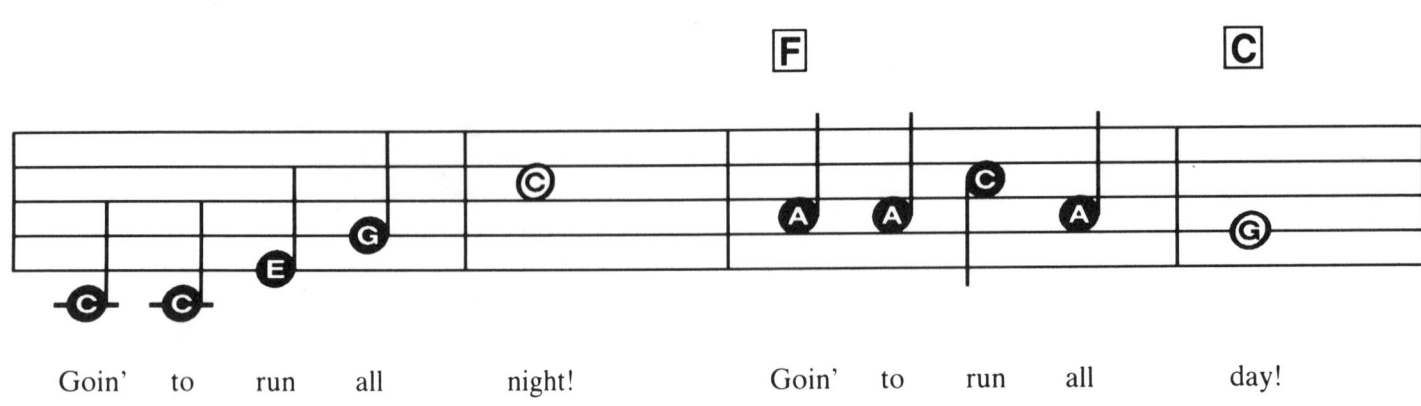
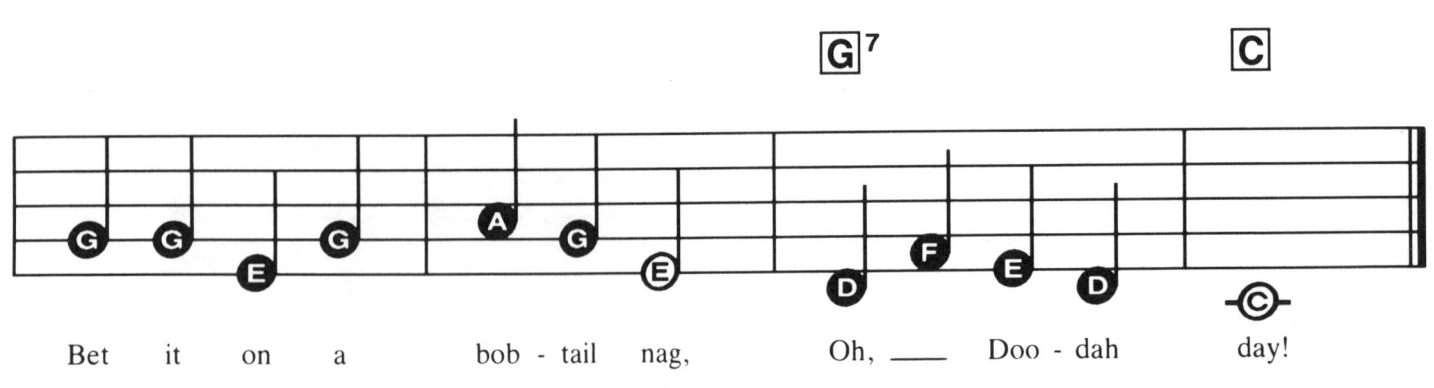

AURA LEE

GREENSLEEVES

Registration 10
Rhythm: Waltz

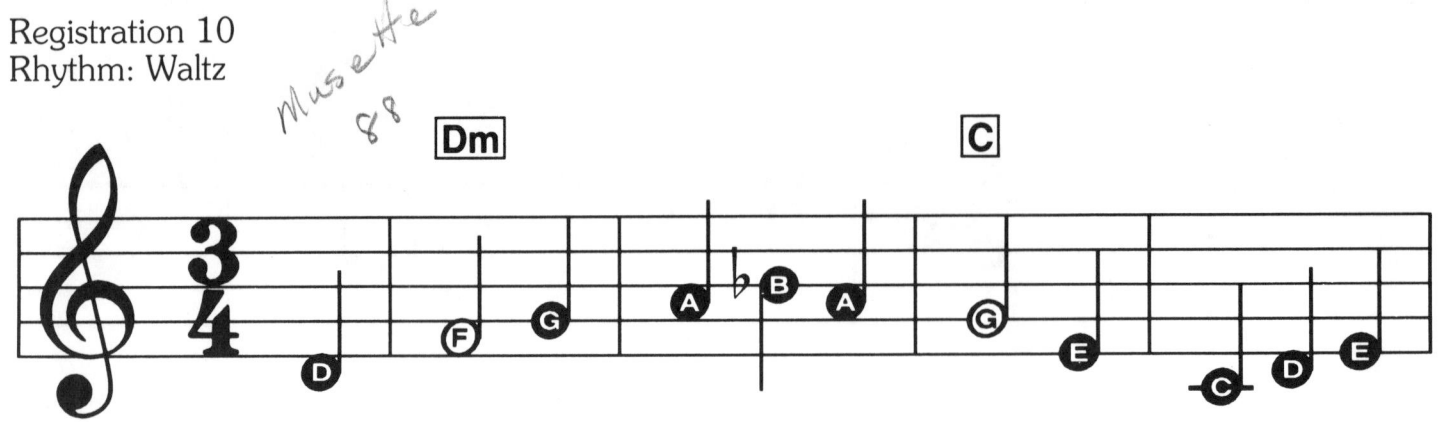
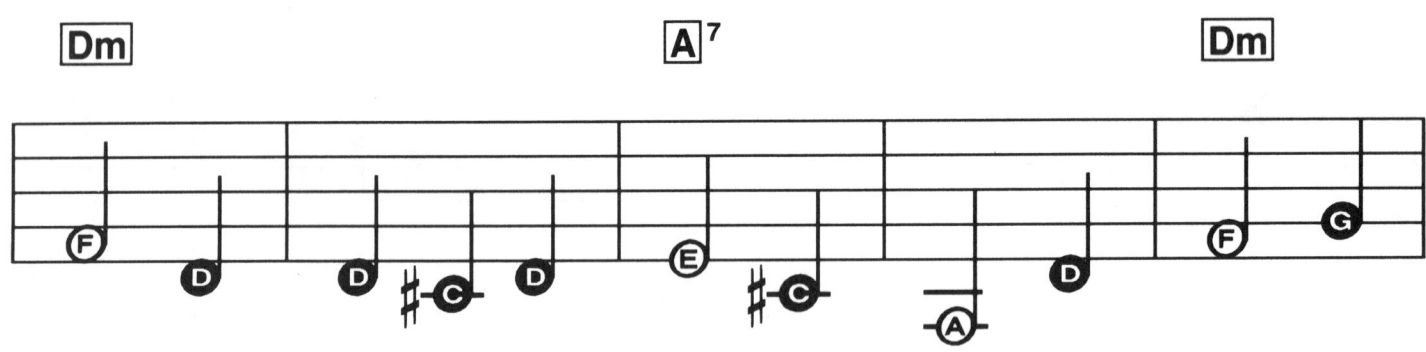
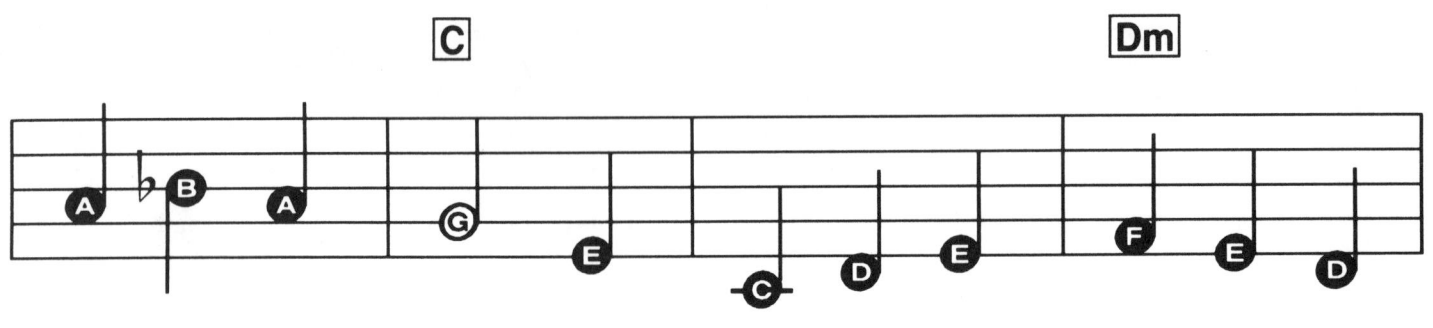
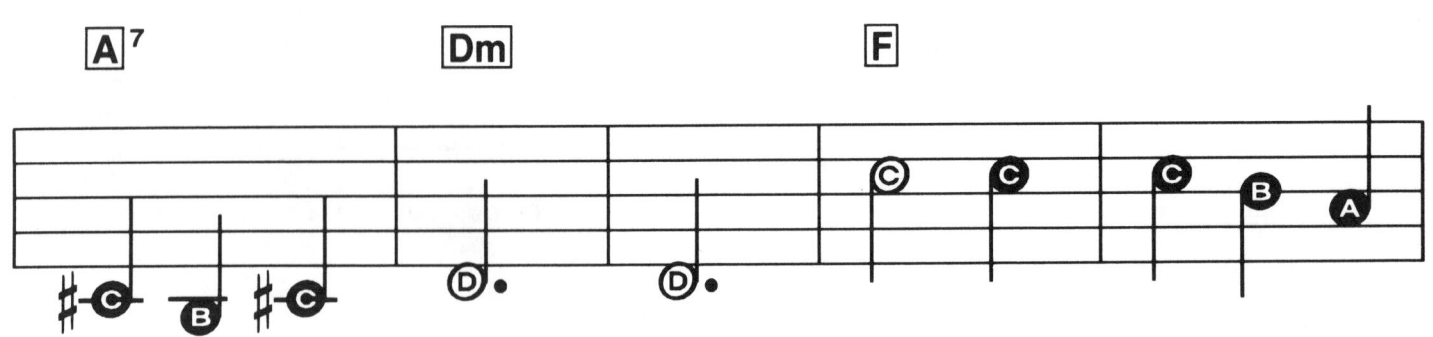

Copyright © 1972 HAL LEONARD CORPORATION
International Copyright Secured All Rights Reserved

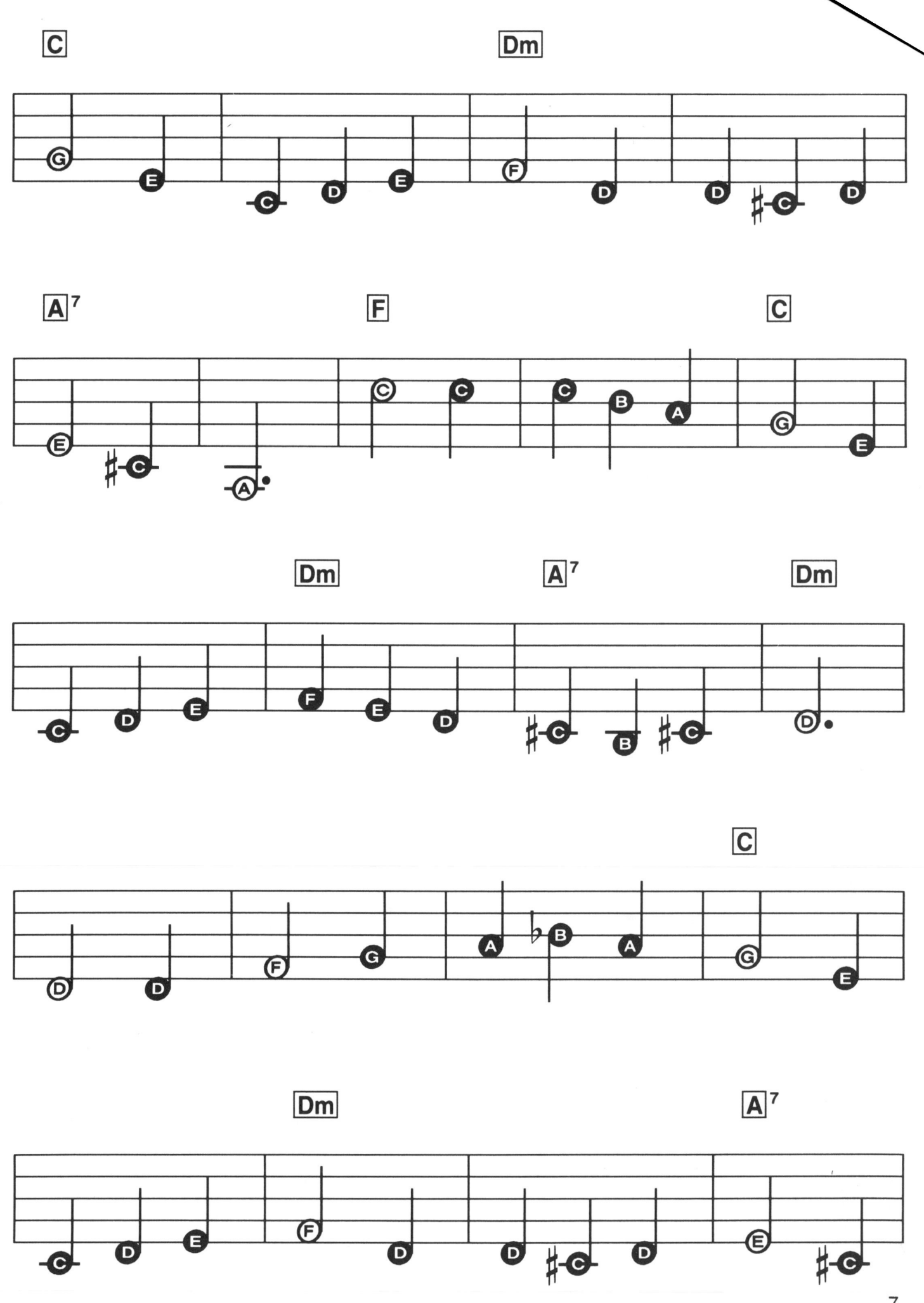

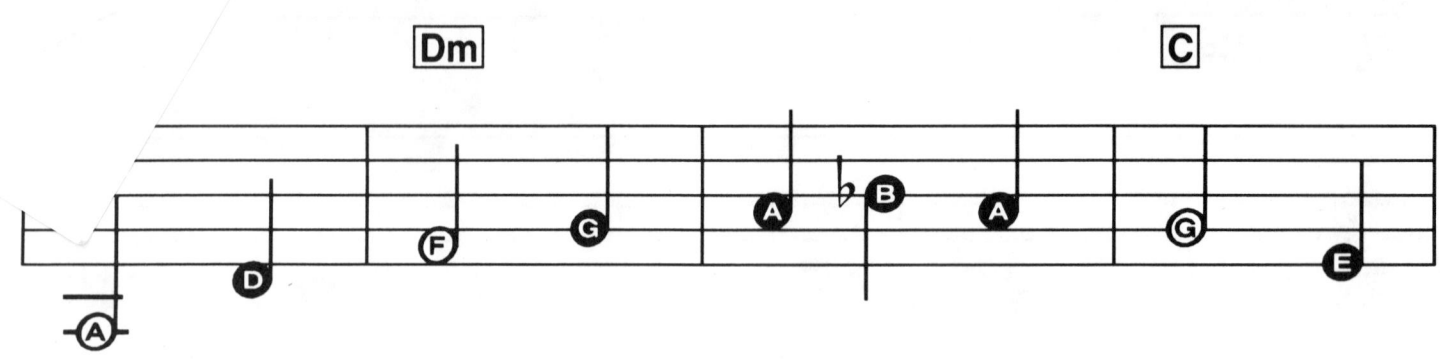

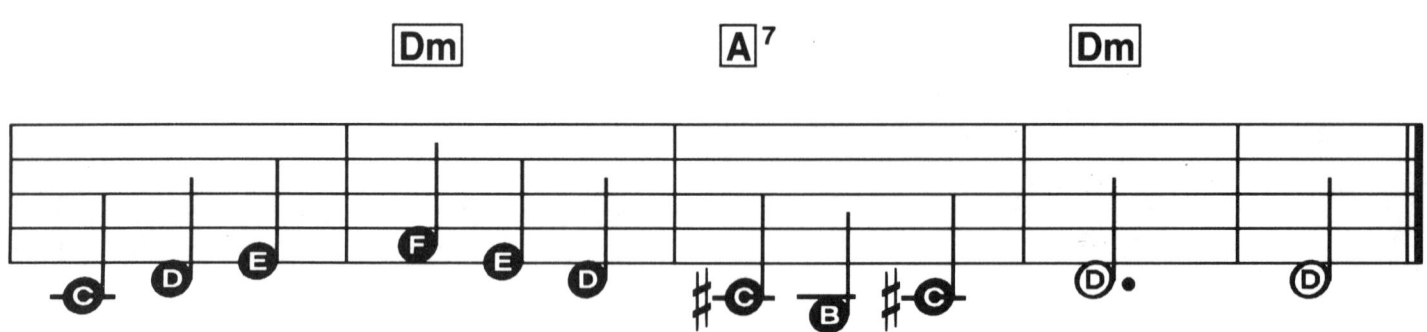

LONG, LONG AGO

Registration 9
Rhythm: Fox Trot or Swing

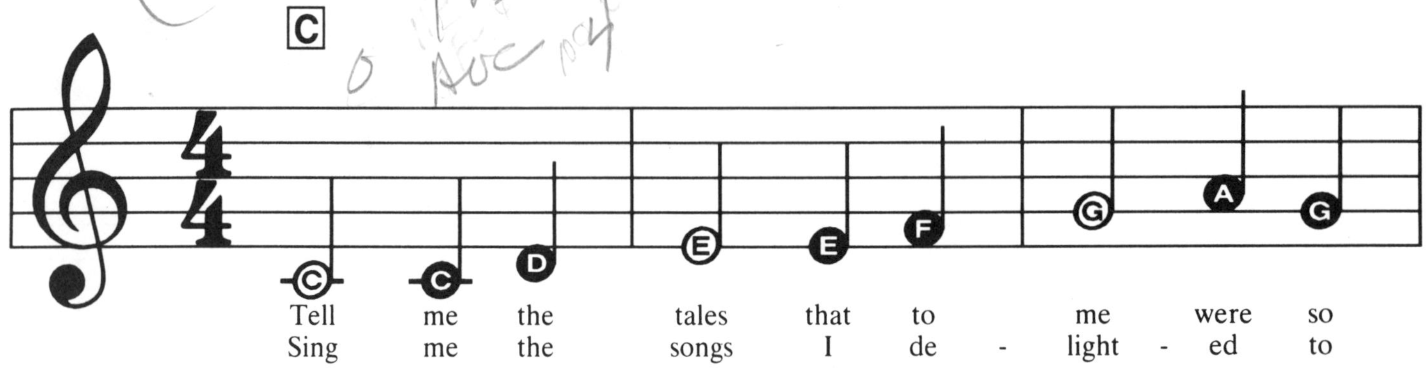

Tell me the tales that to me were so
Sing me the songs I de-light-ed to

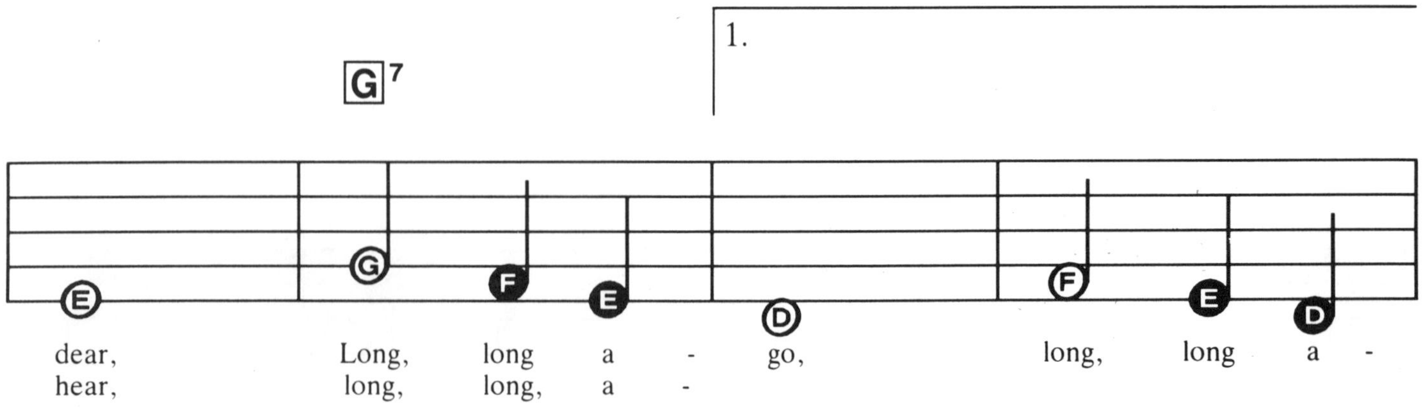

dear,   Long, long a - go,   long, long a -
hear,   long, long, a -

Copyright © 1972 HAL LEONARD CORPORATION
International Copyright Secured   All Rights Reserved

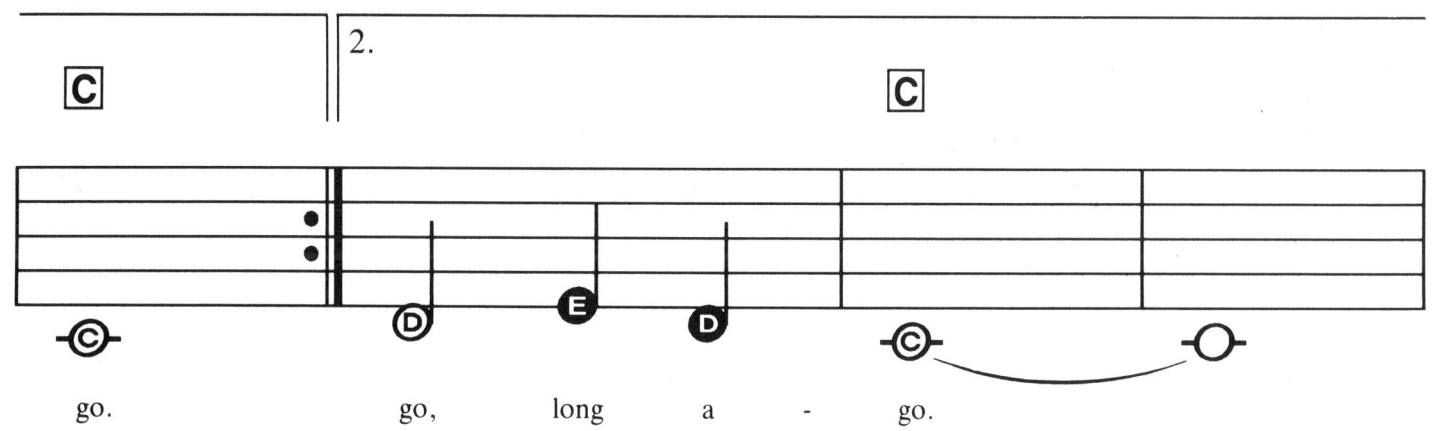
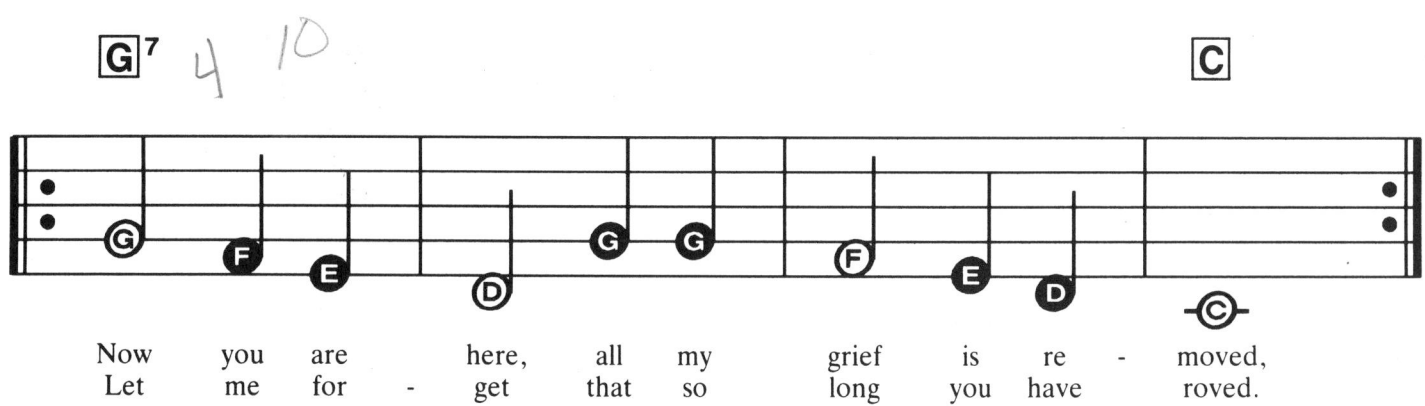
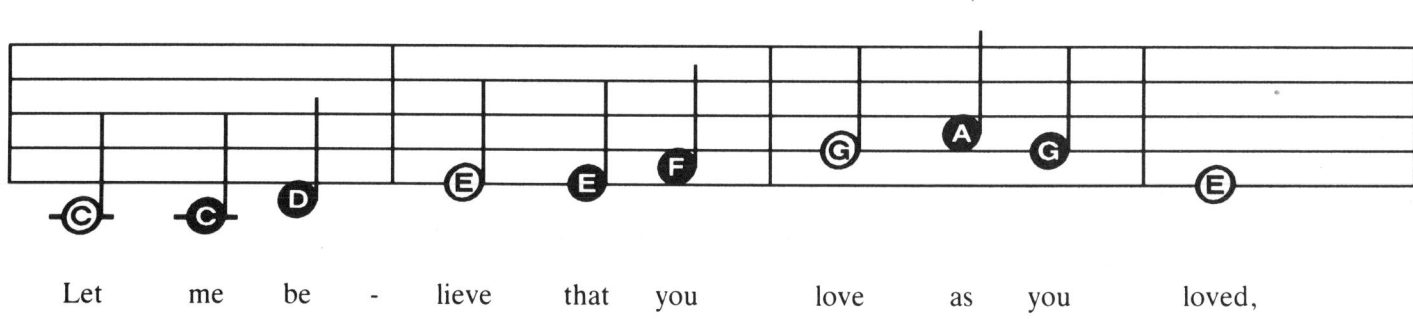
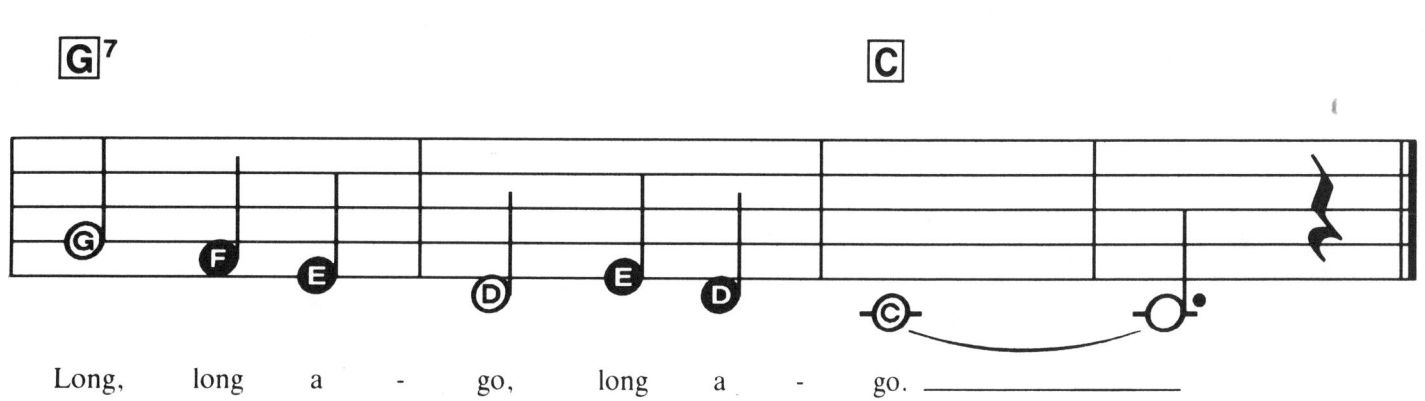

TALES FROM THE VIENNA WOODS

Registration 3
Rhythm: Waltz

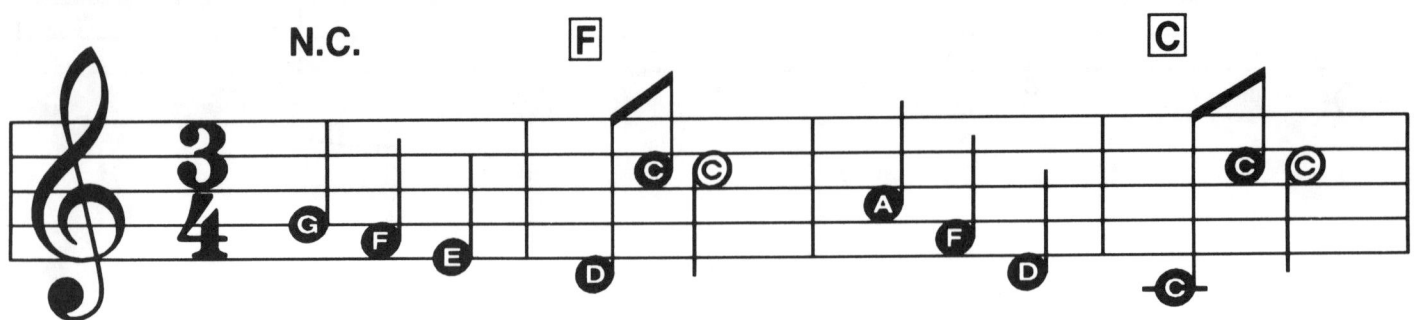
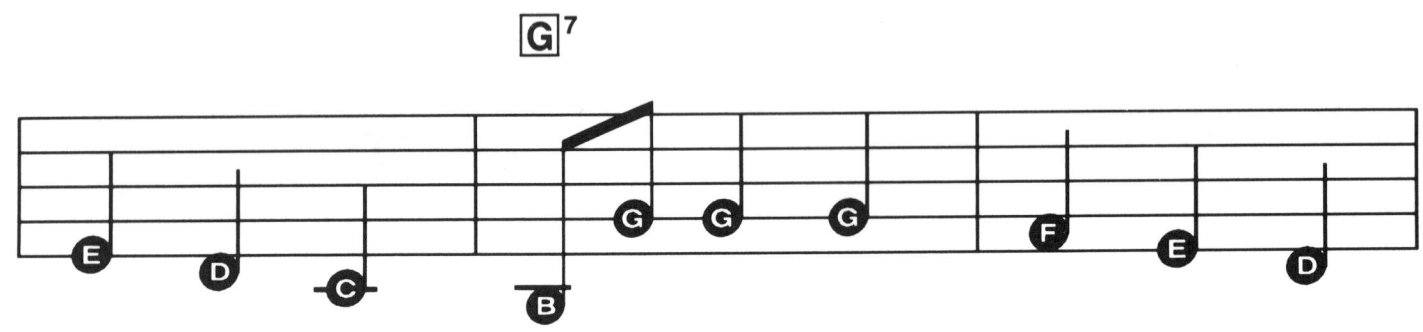
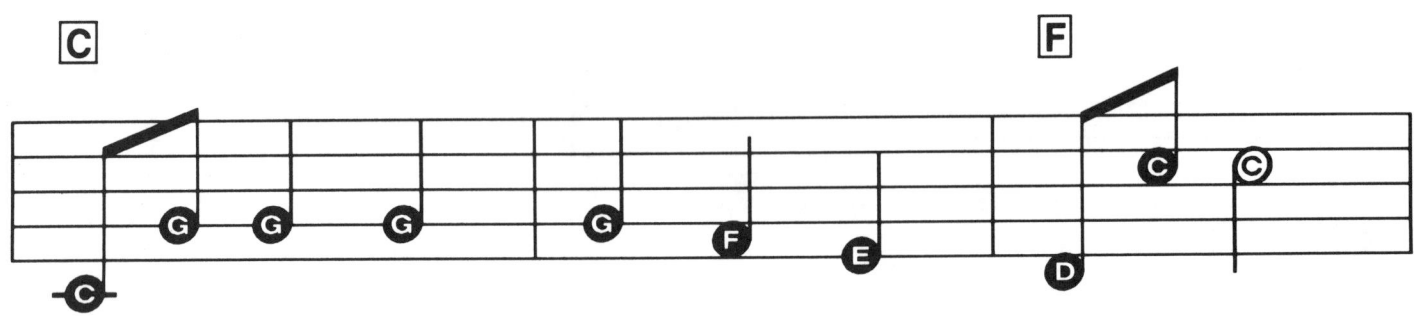
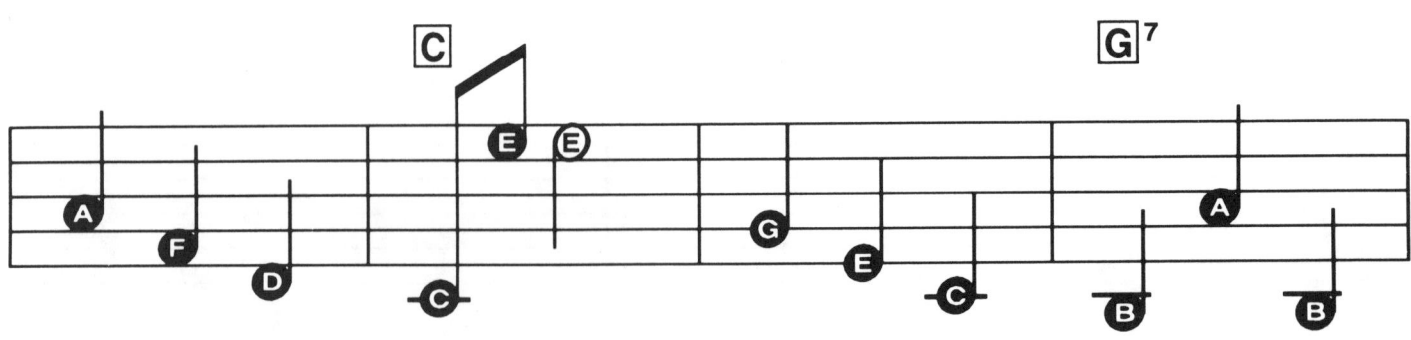

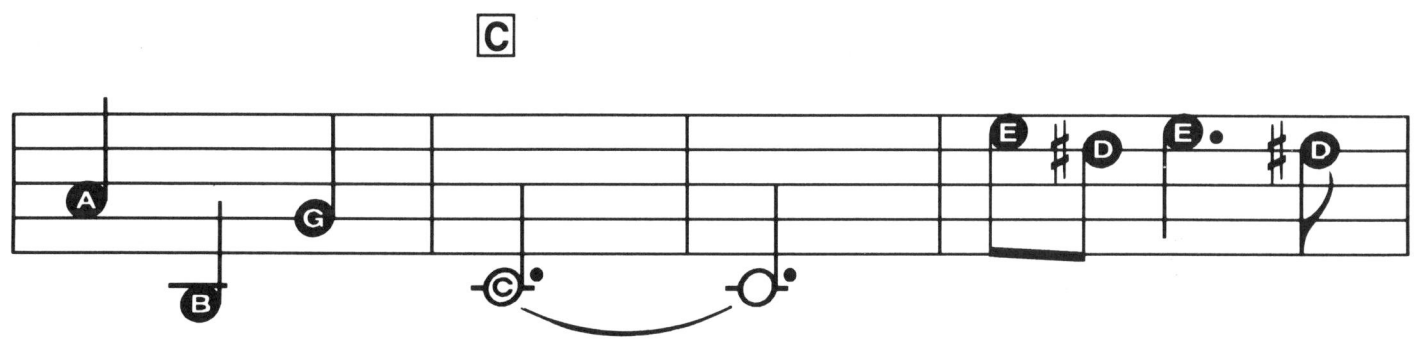
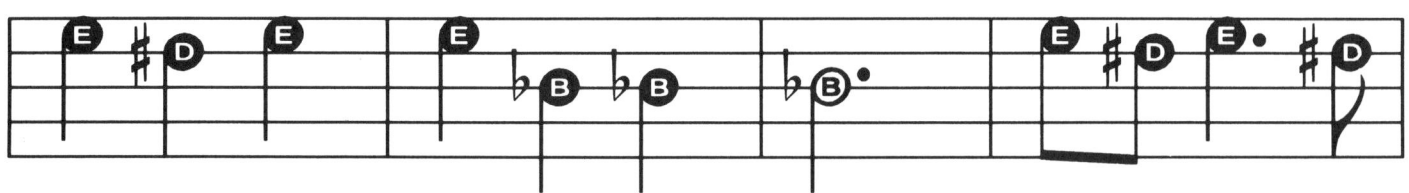
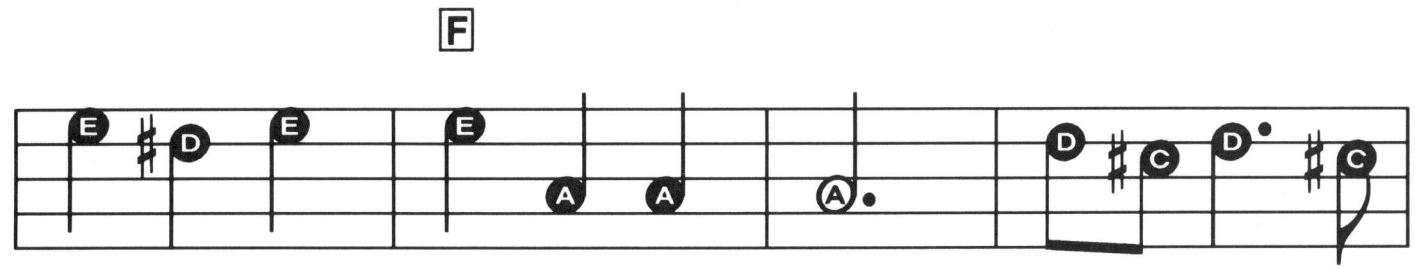
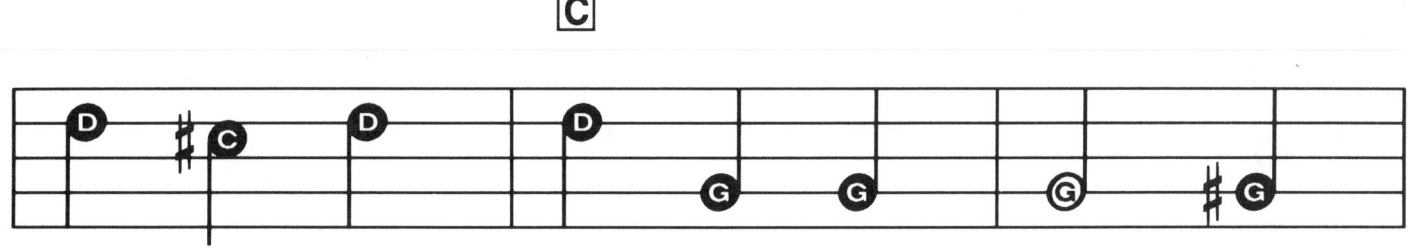
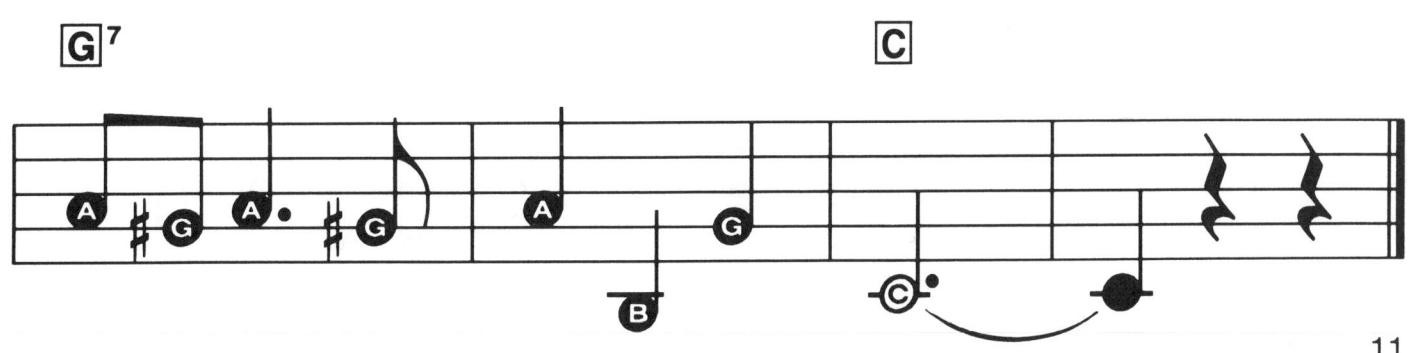

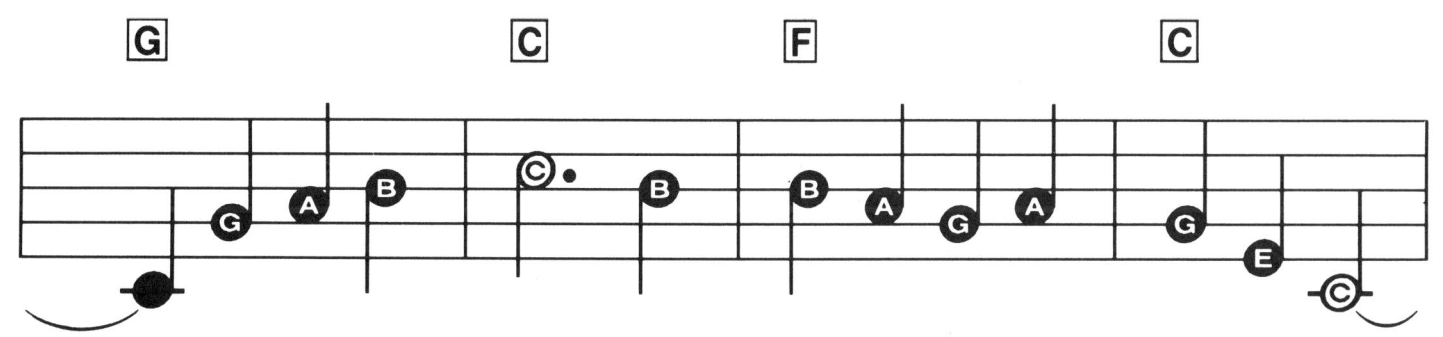
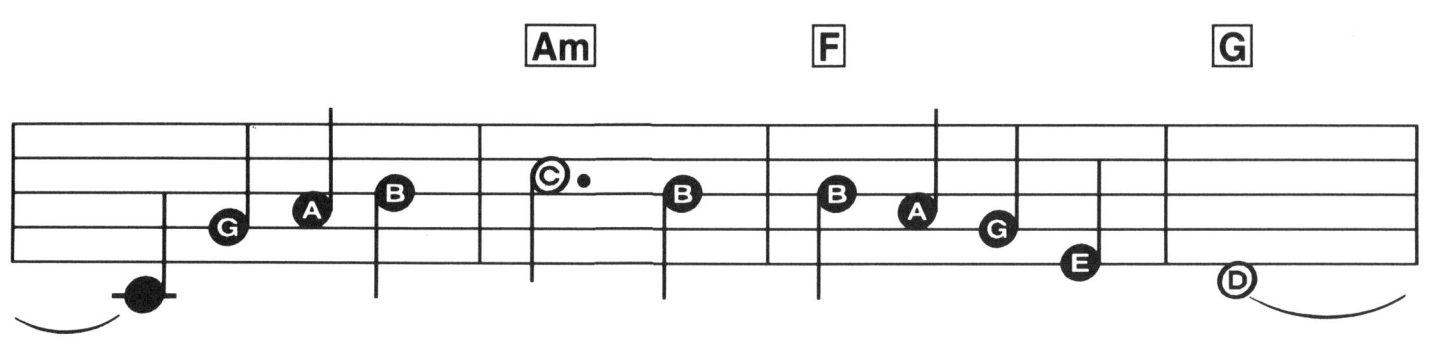
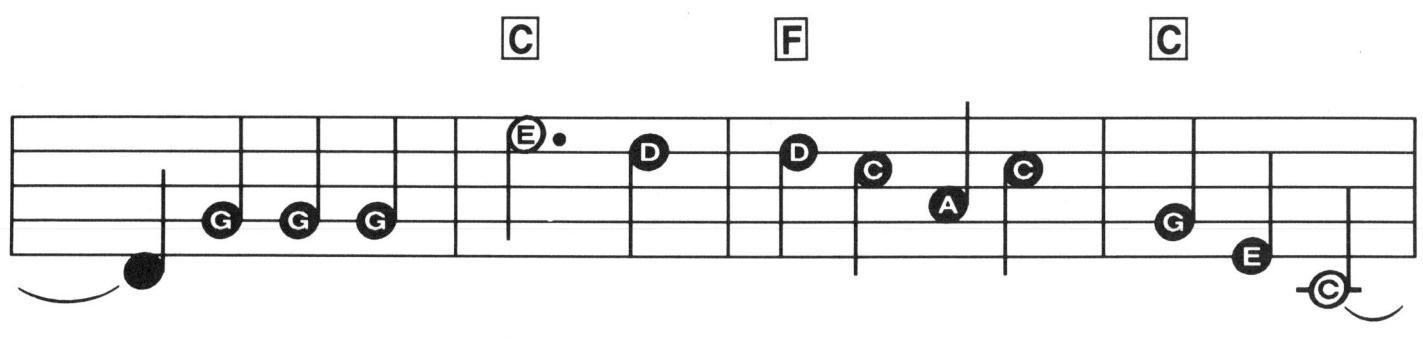
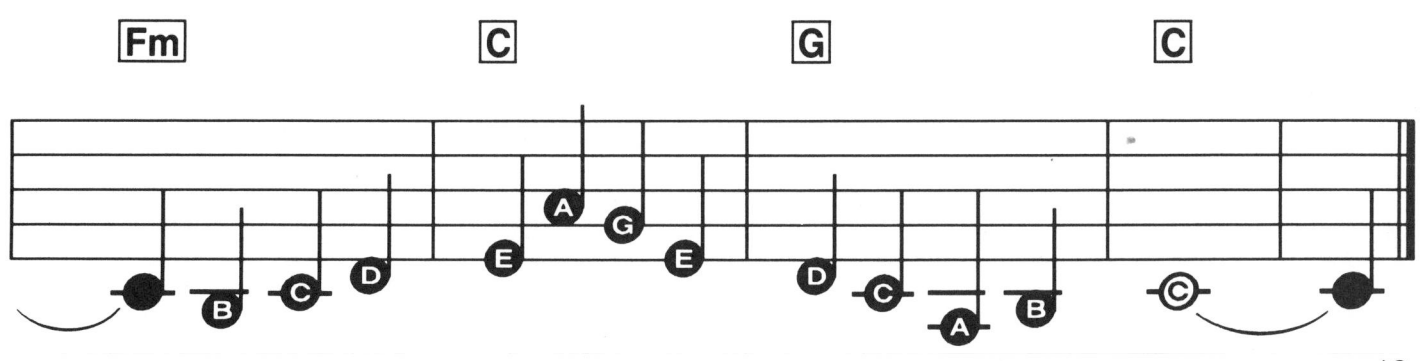

MY WILD IRISH ROSE

Registration 2
Rhythm: Waltz

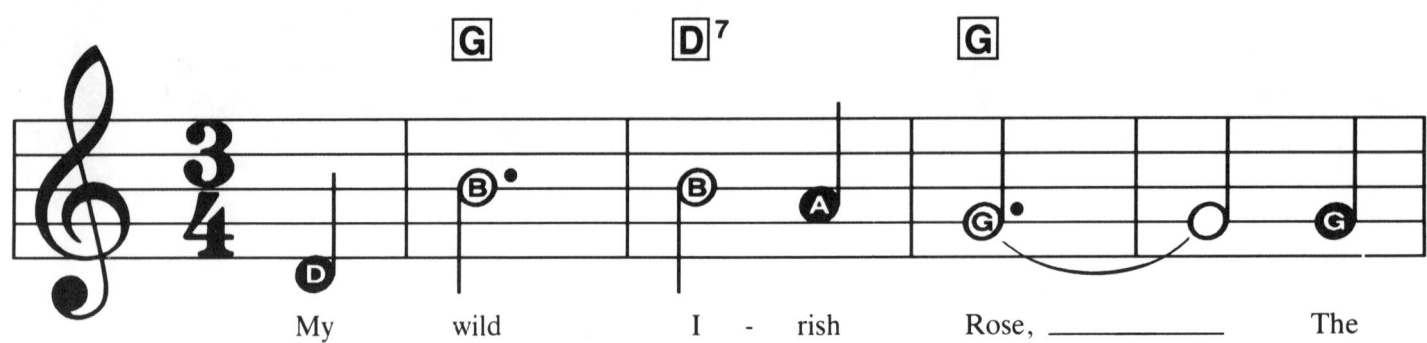

My wild I - rish Rose, _____ The

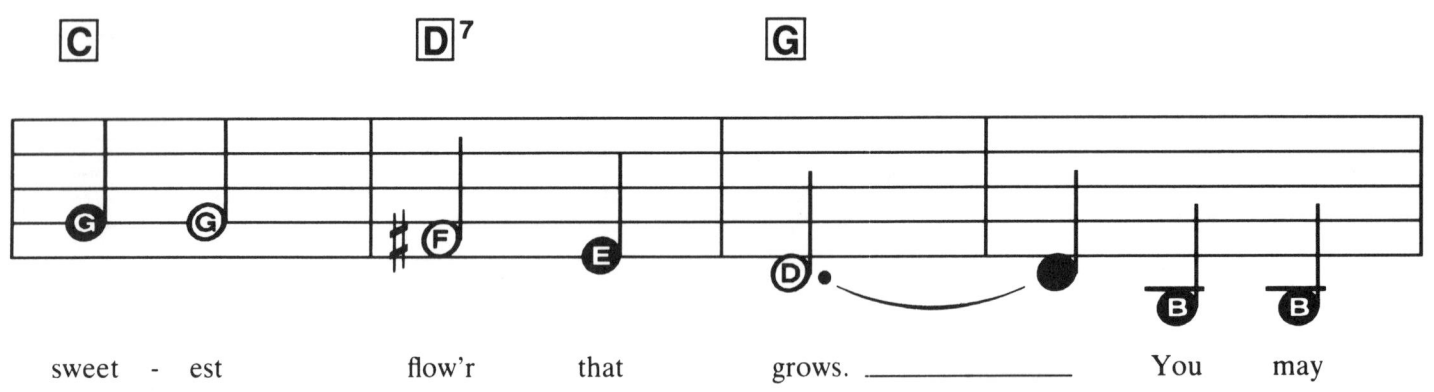

sweet - est flow'r that grows. _____ You may

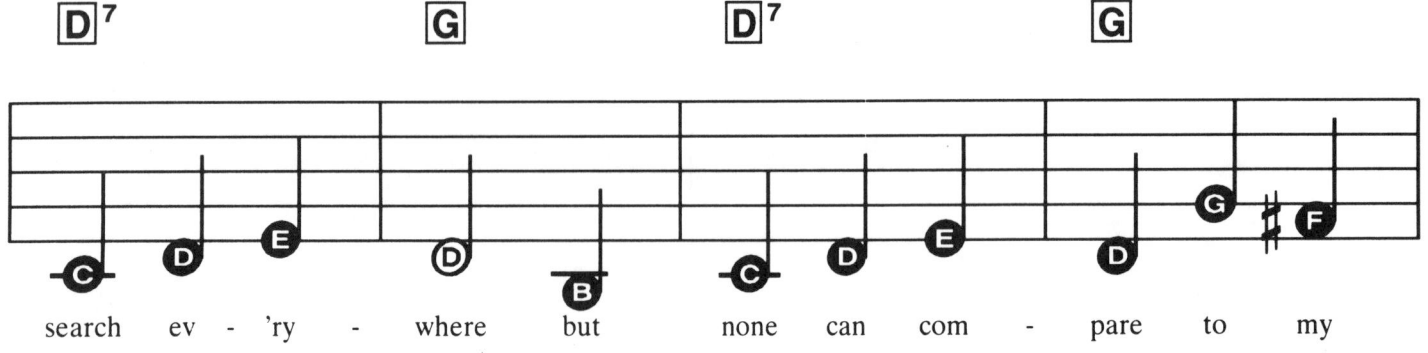

search ev - 'ry - where but none can com - pare to my

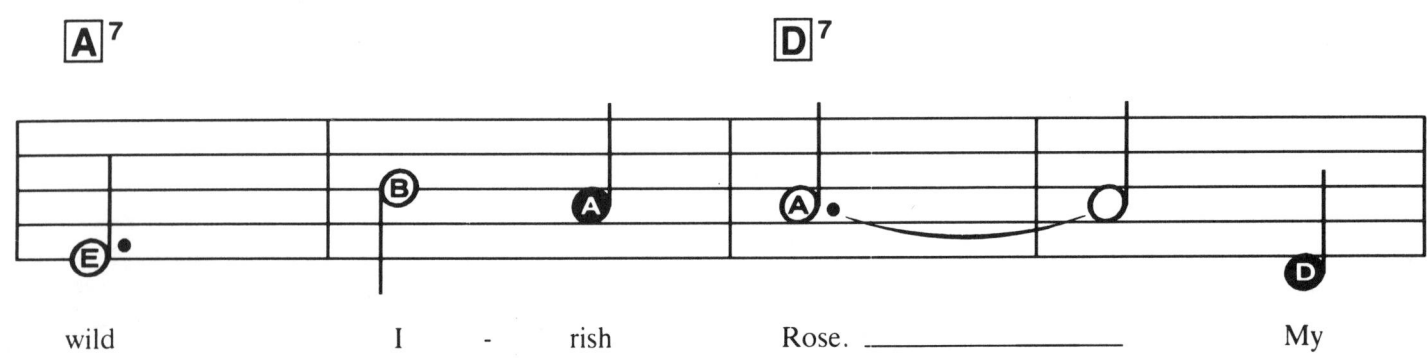

wild I - rish Rose. _____ My

Copyright © 1972 HAL LEONARD CORPORATION
International Copyright Secured   All Rights Reserved

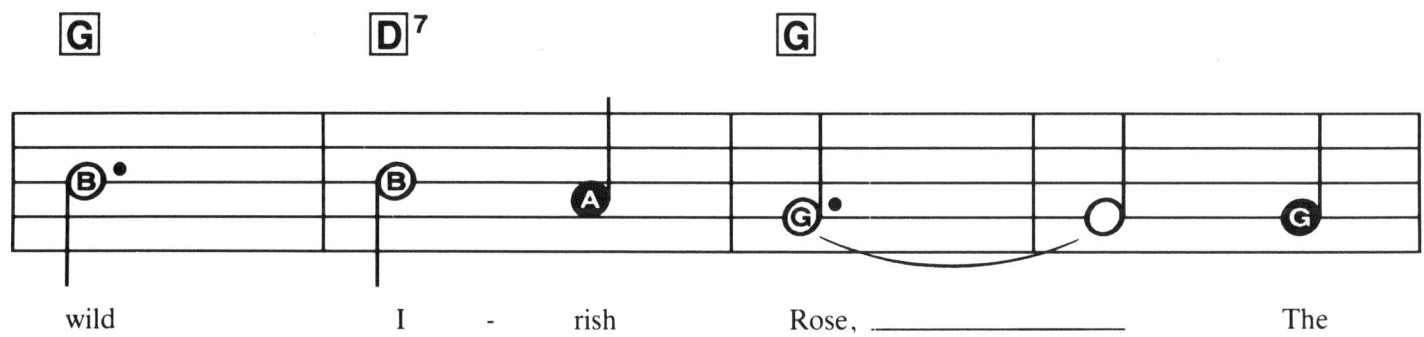
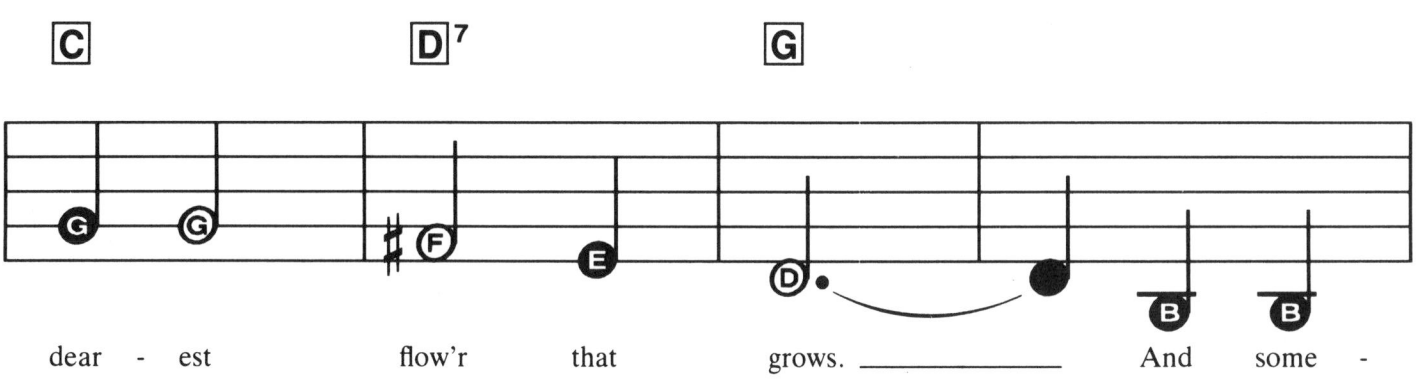
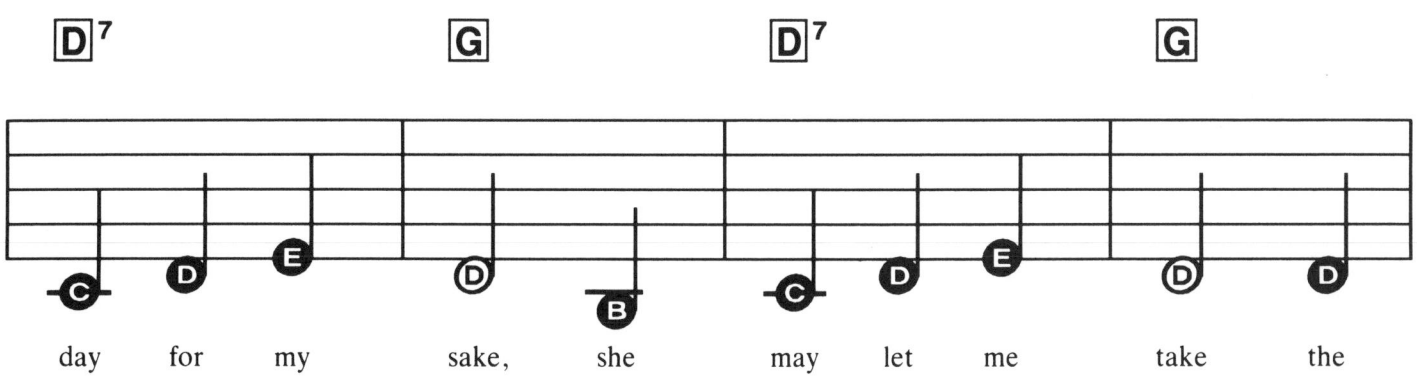
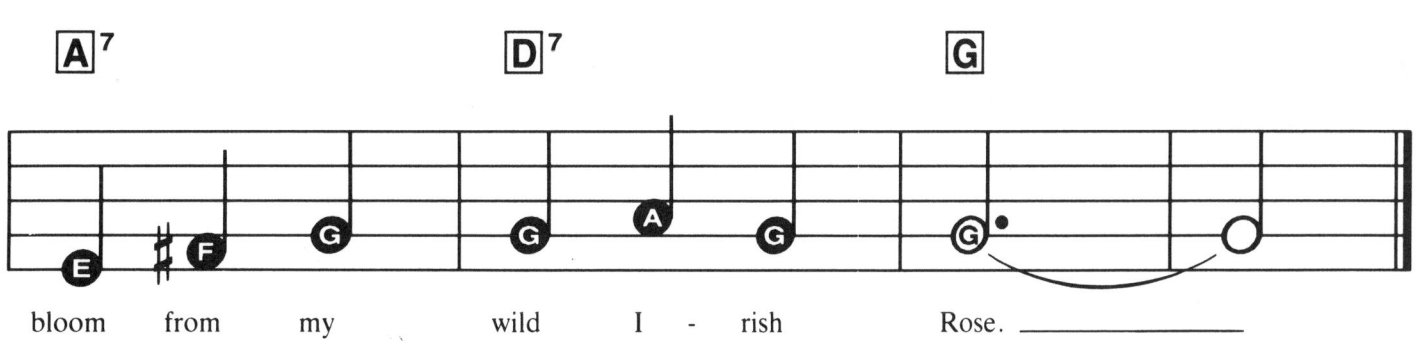

LAVENDER'S BLUE

Registration 3
Rhythm: Fox Trot or Swing

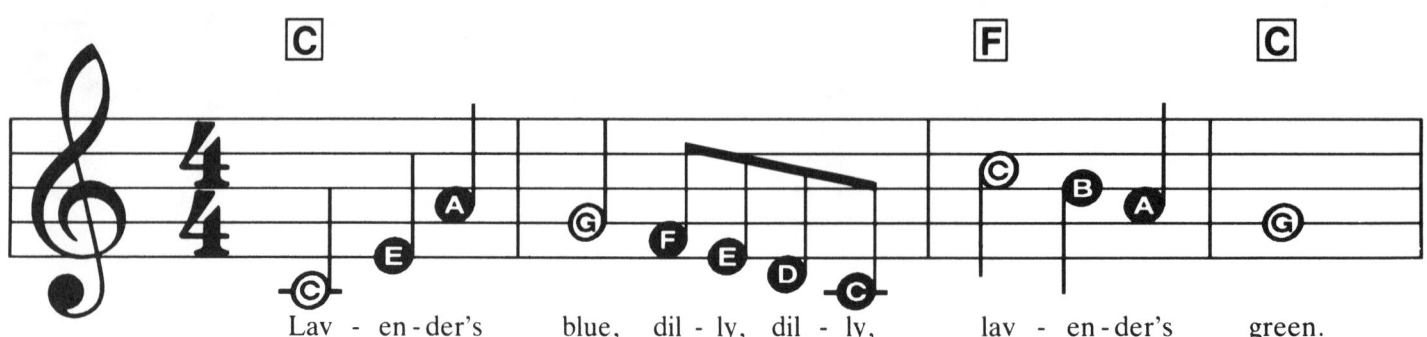

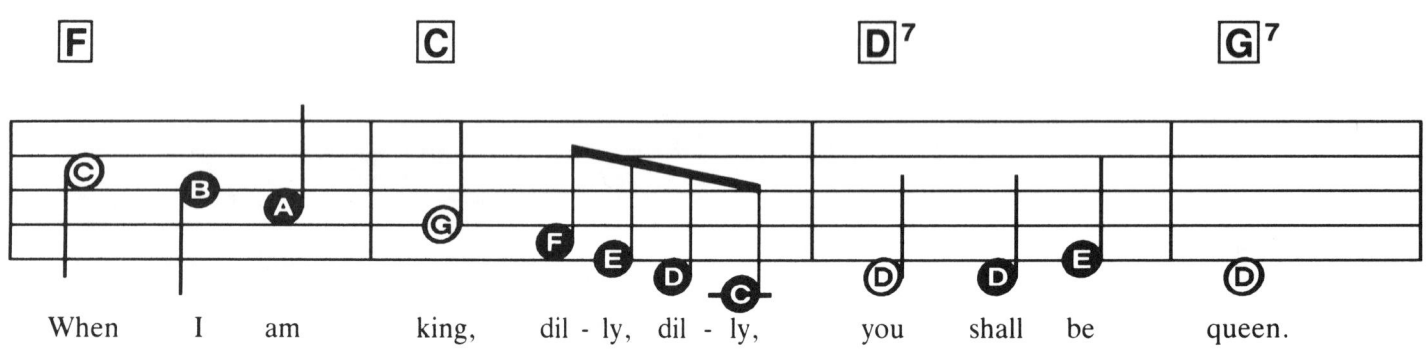

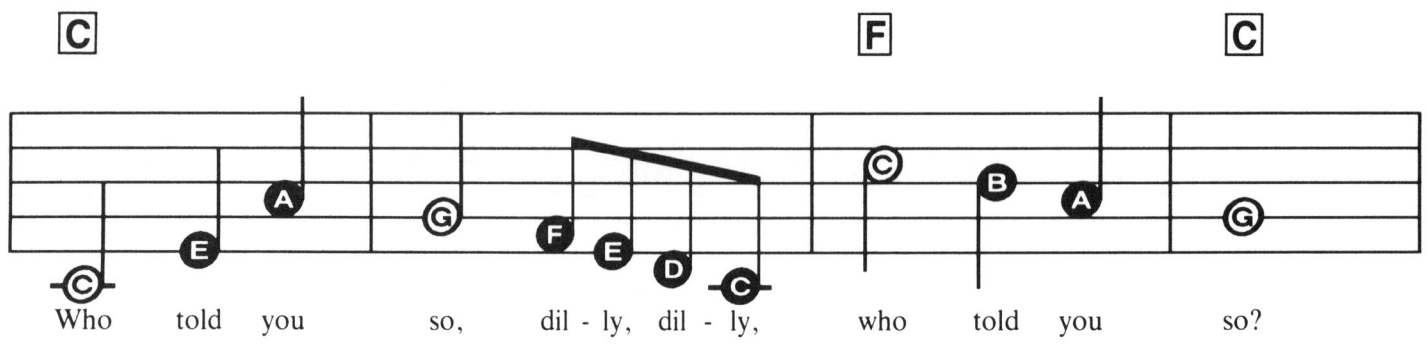

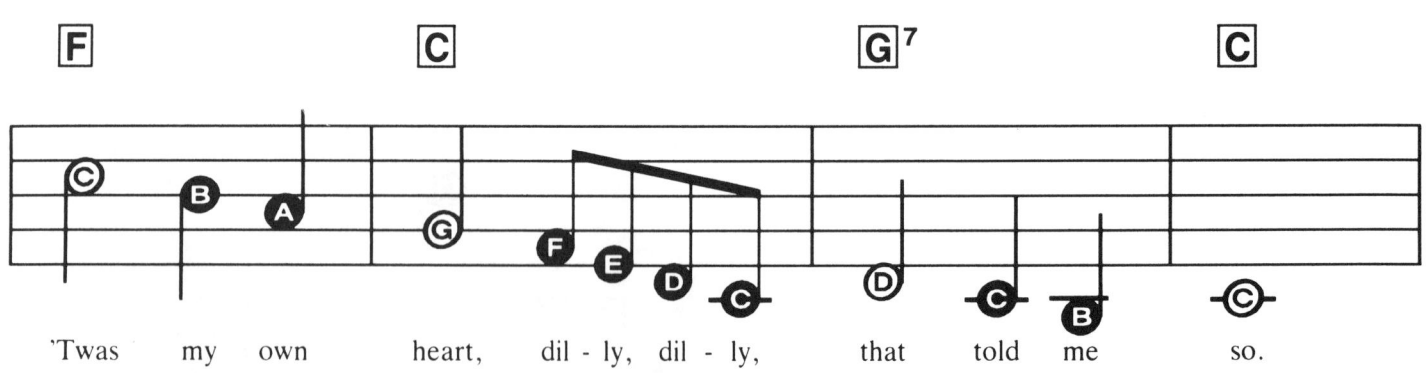

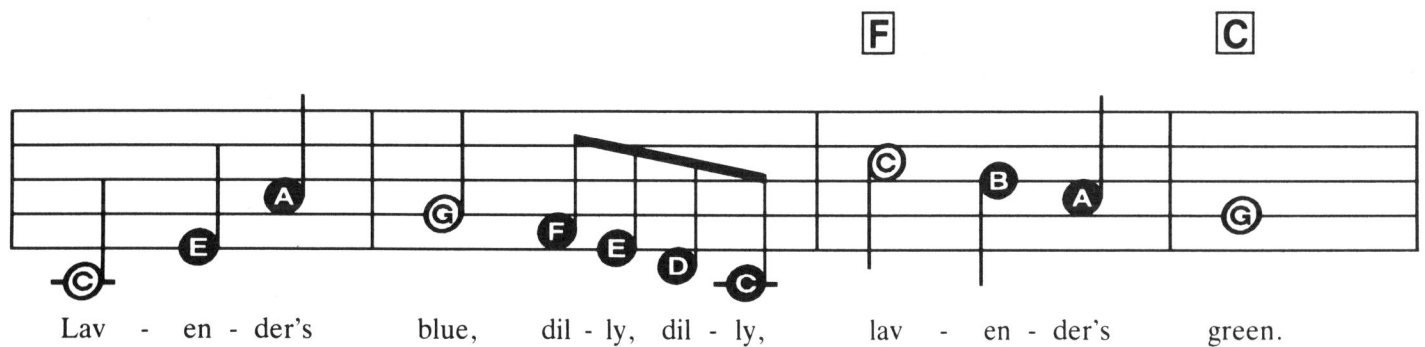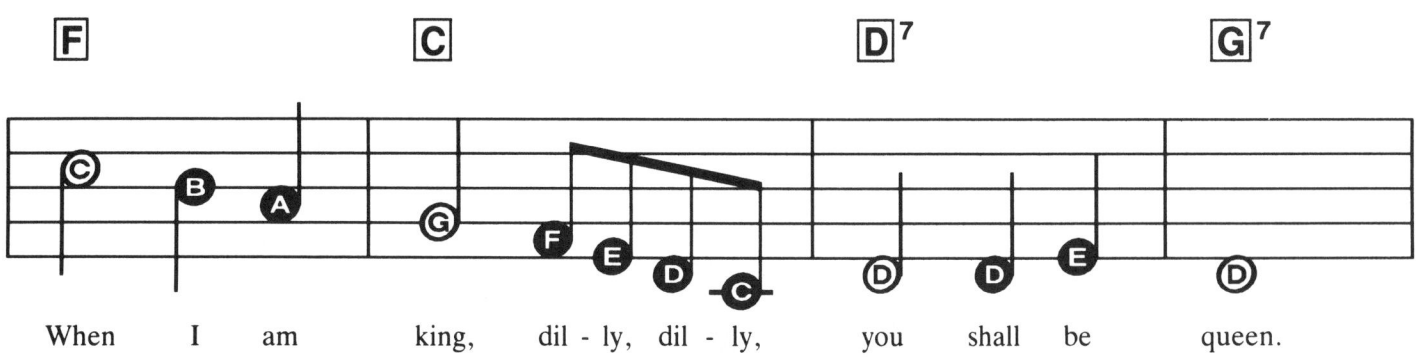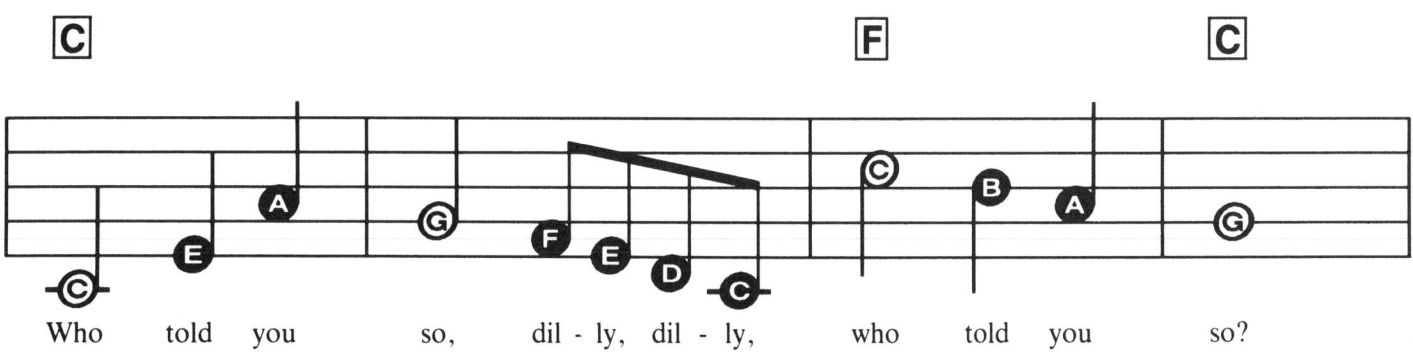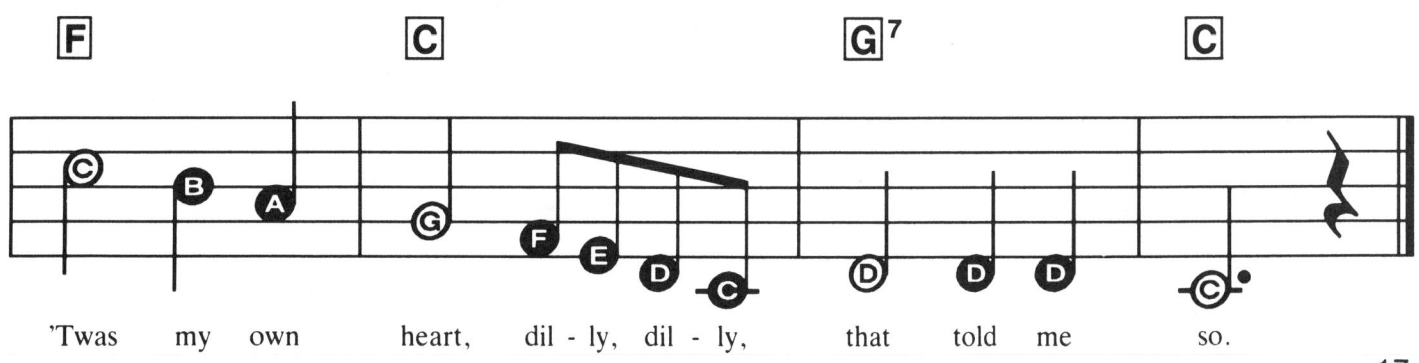

MICHAEL, ROW THE BOAT ASHORE

Registration 7
Rhythm: Rock or 8 Beat

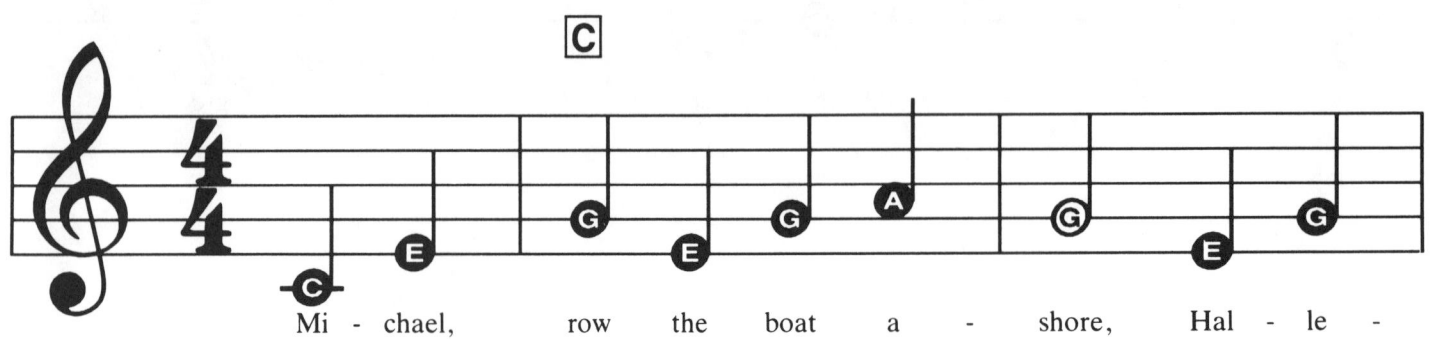
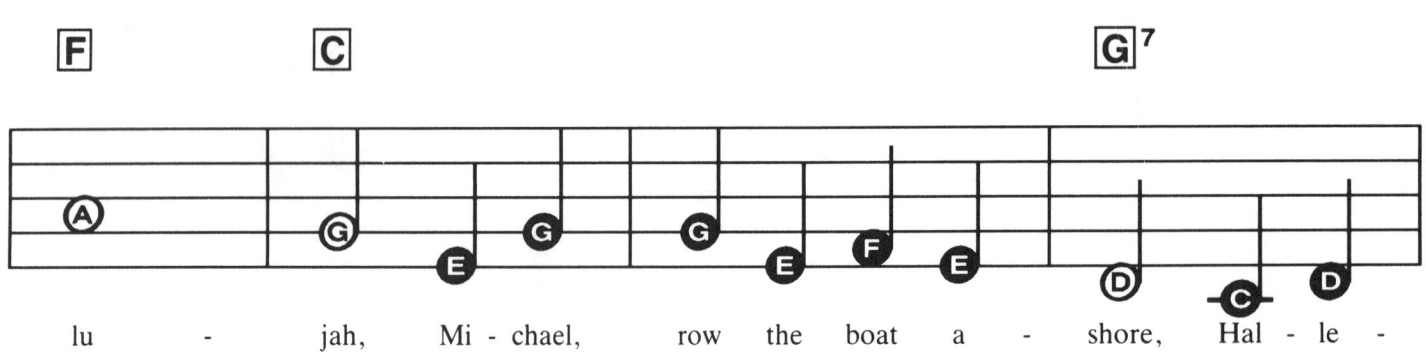
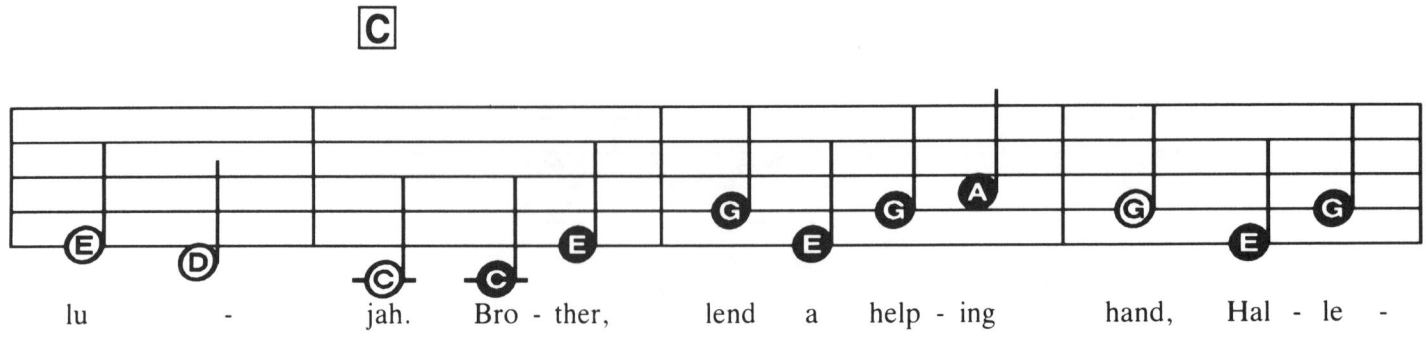
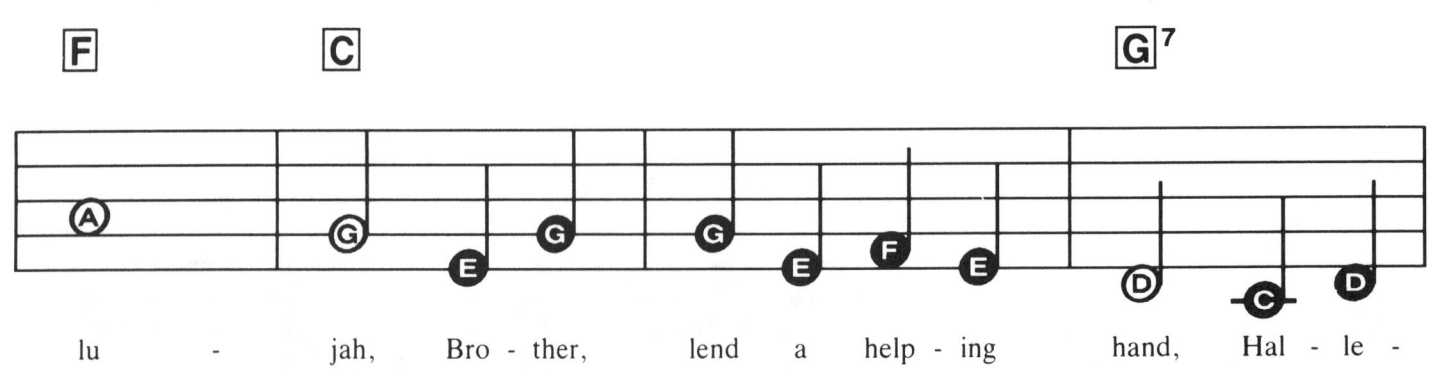

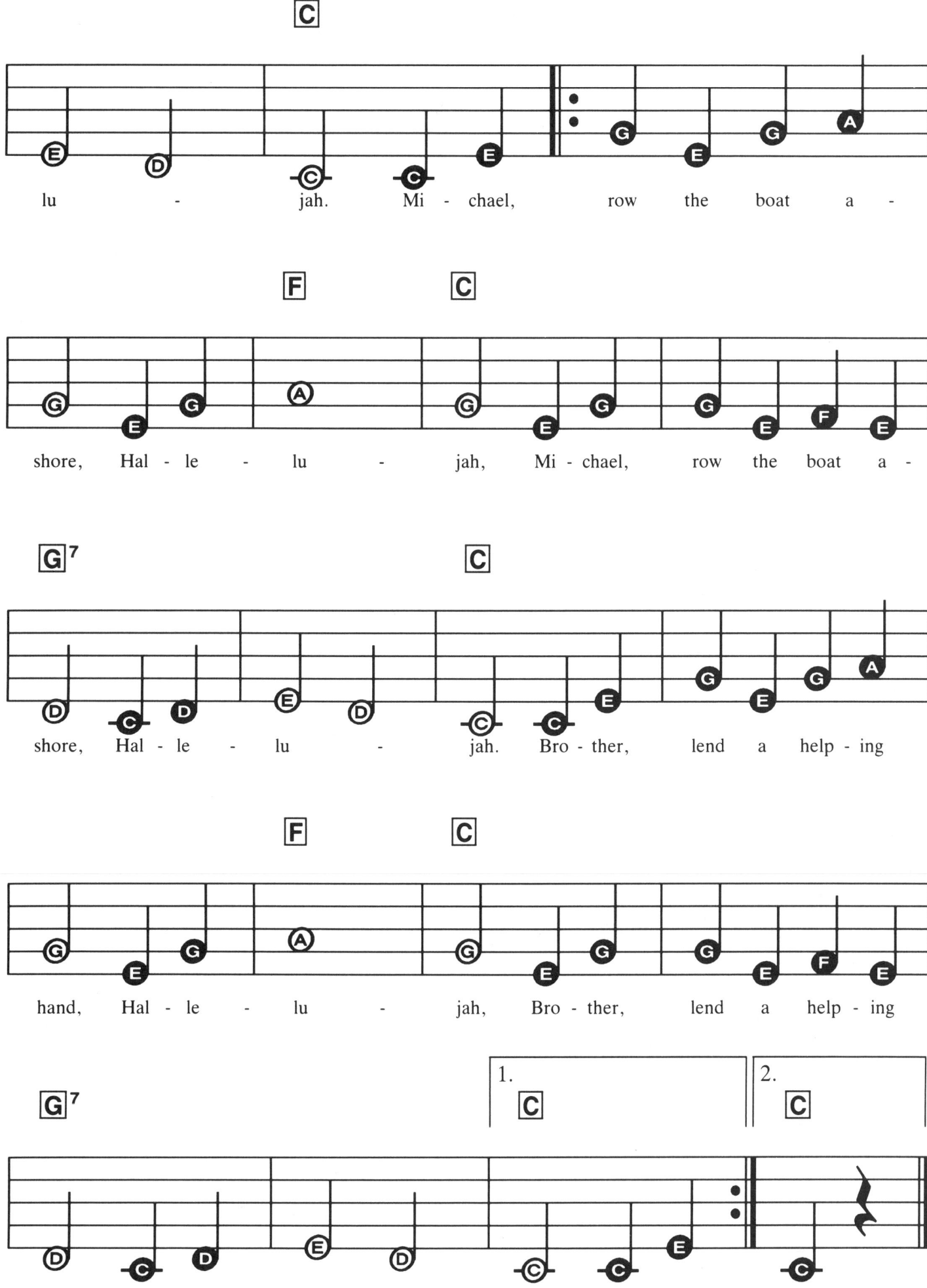

CARNIVAL OF VENICE

Registration 4
Rhythm: Waltz

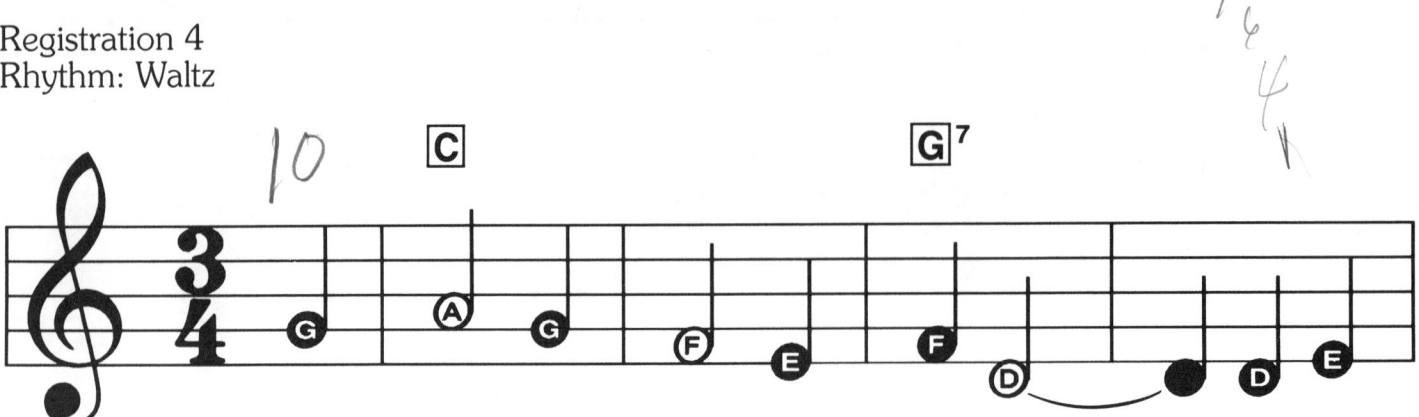

My gon - do - la is sway - ing ____ in a

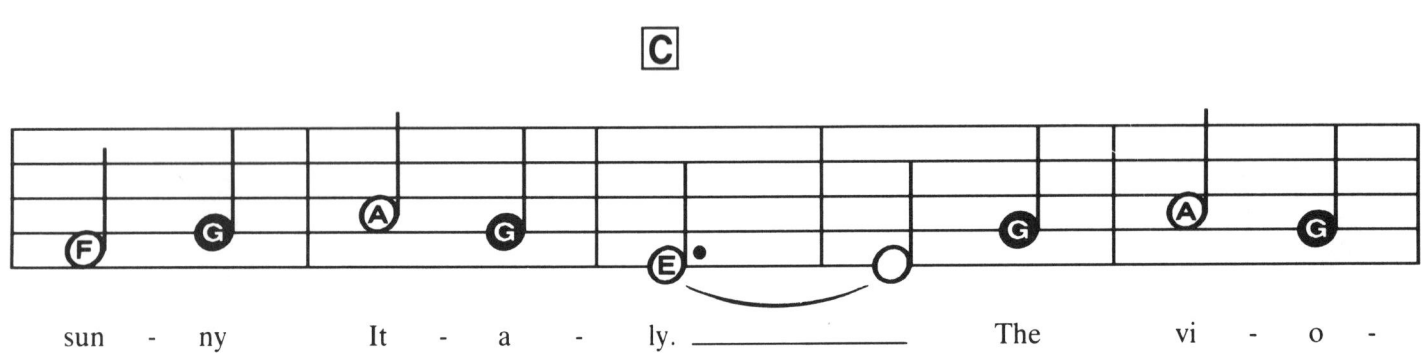

sun - ny It - a - ly. ____ The vi - o -

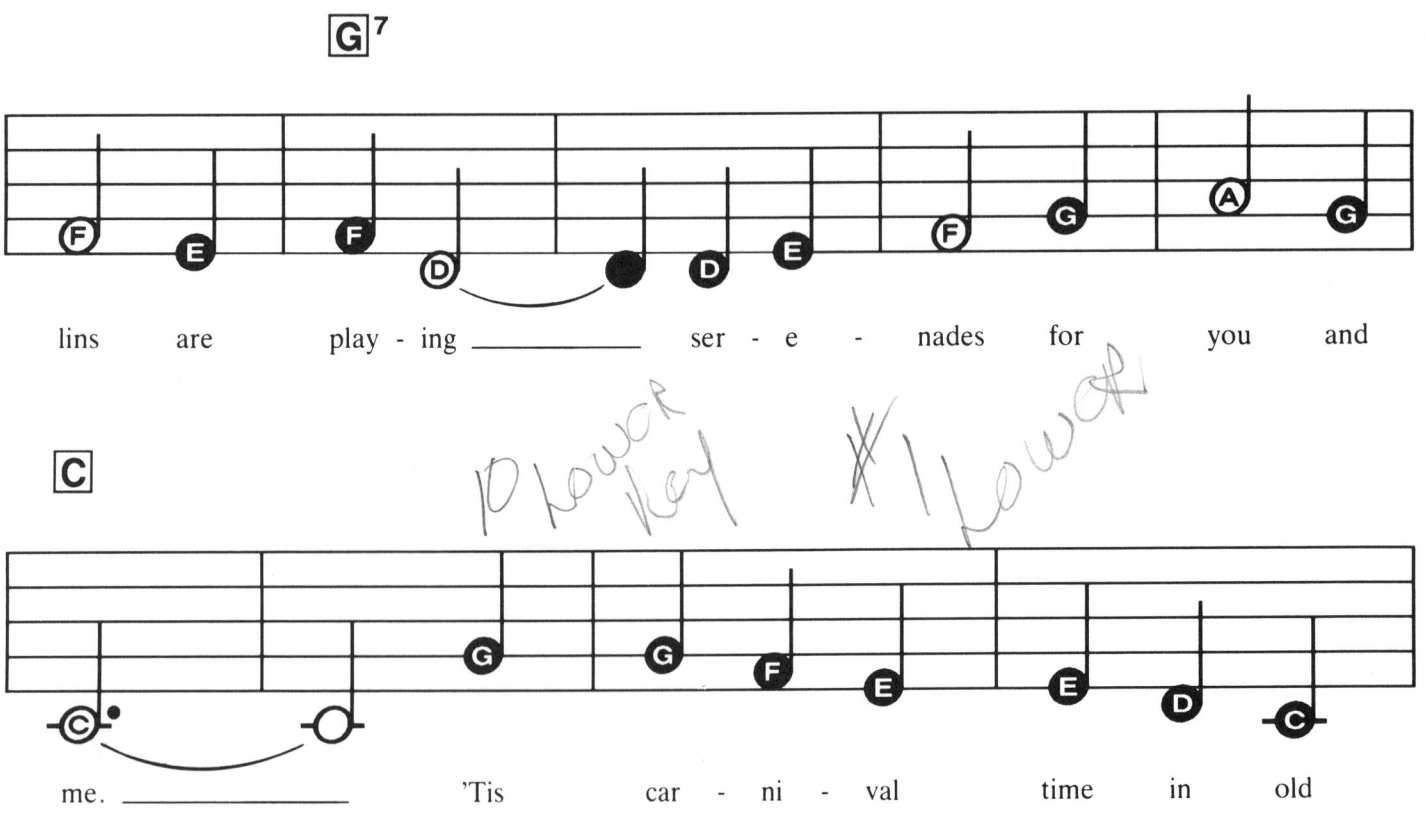

lins are play - ing ____ ser - e - nades for you and

me. ____ 'Tis car - ni - val time in old

Copyright © 1972 HAL LEONARD CORPORATION
International Copyright Secured   All Rights Reserved

G7
Ven - ice ___ and the mu - sic is sub -
C
lime. ___ I hope that it nev - er will
G7
cease; ___ Play it through time af - ter
C
G7
time. ___ My gon - do - la is sway - ing ___
C
___ in a sun - ny It - a - ly. ___

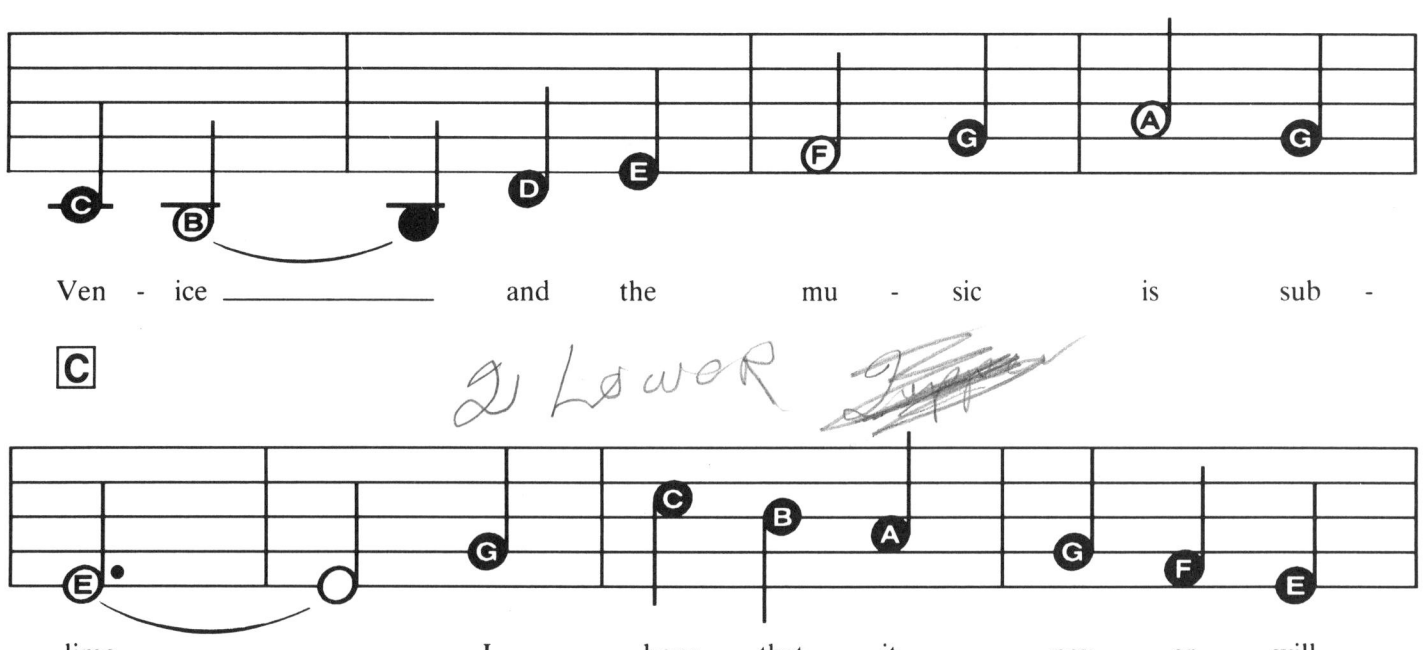

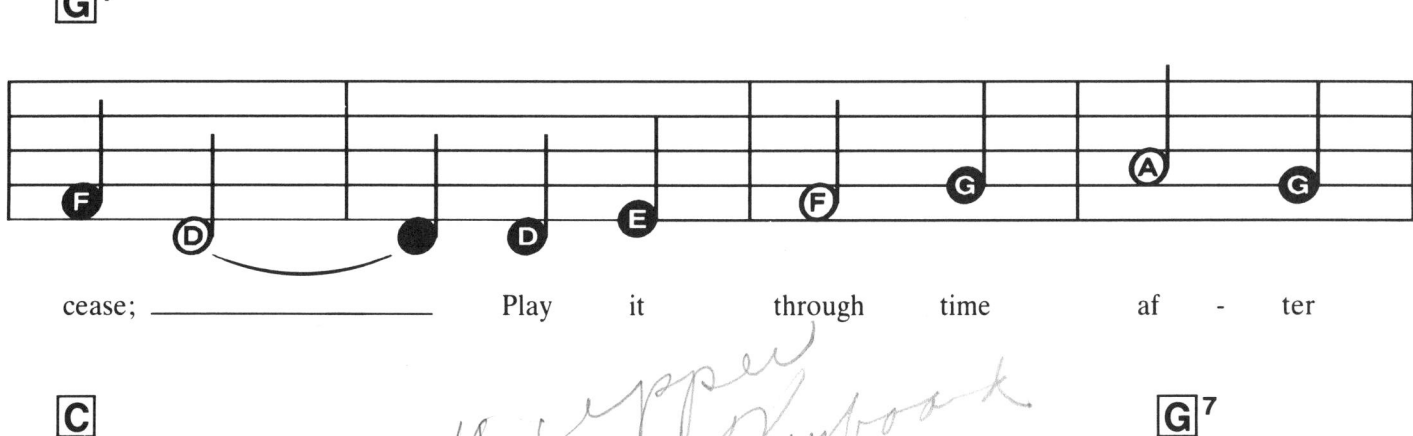

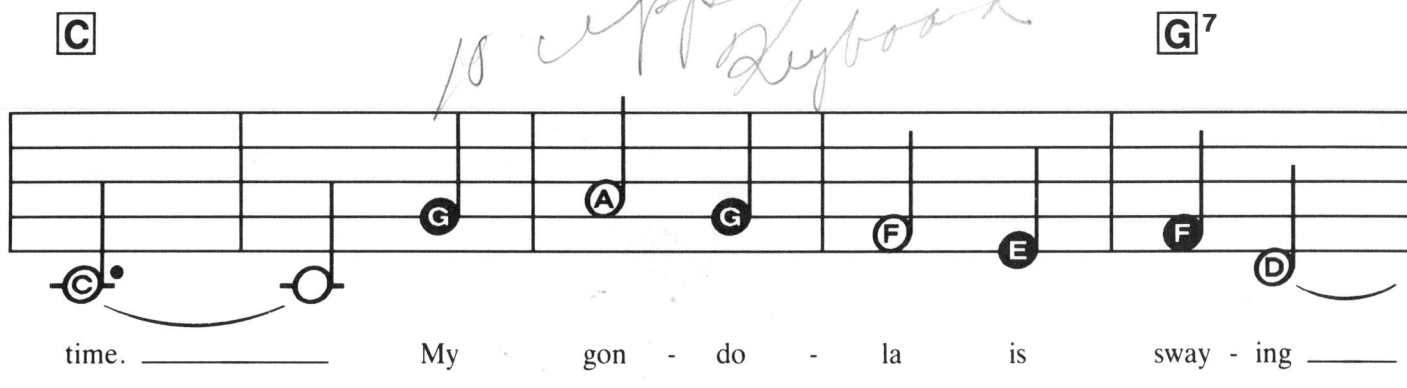

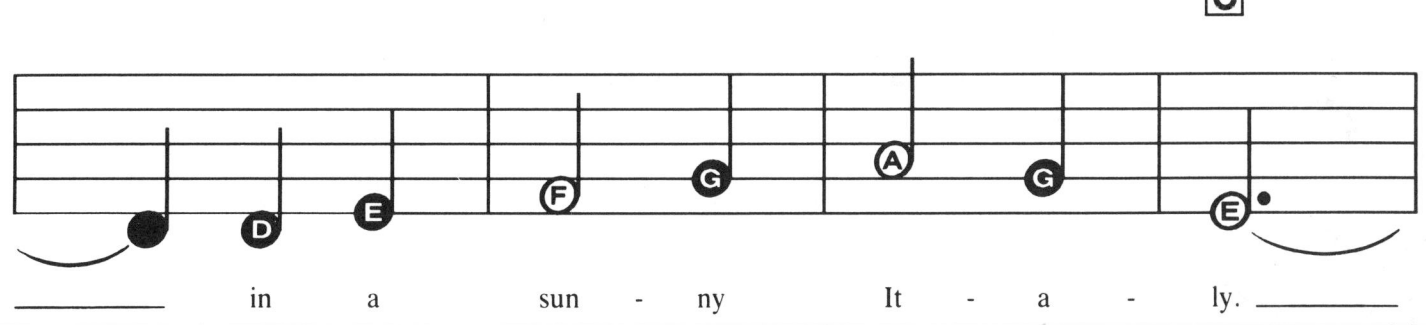

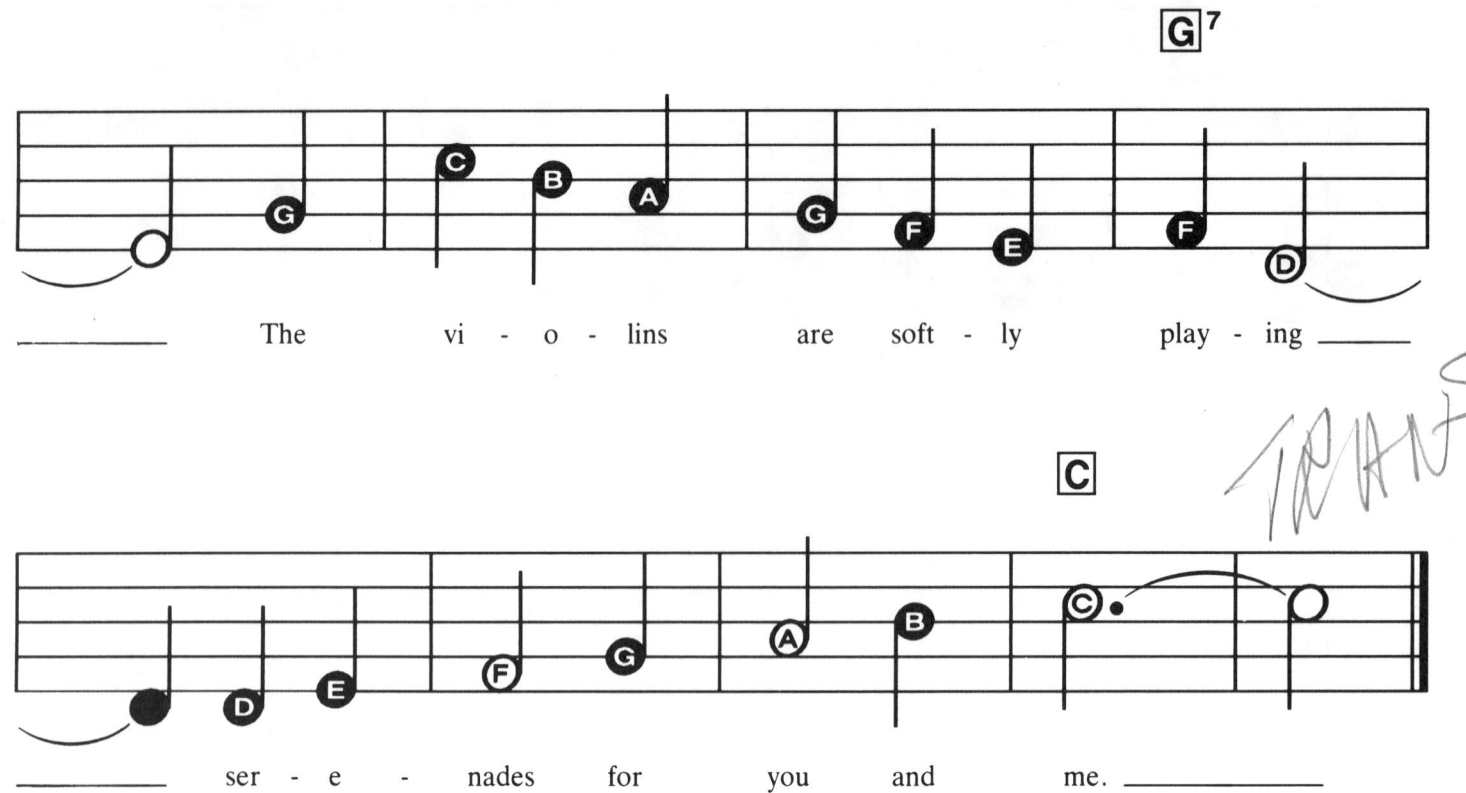

DIXIE

Registration 7
Rhythm: Fox Trot or Swing

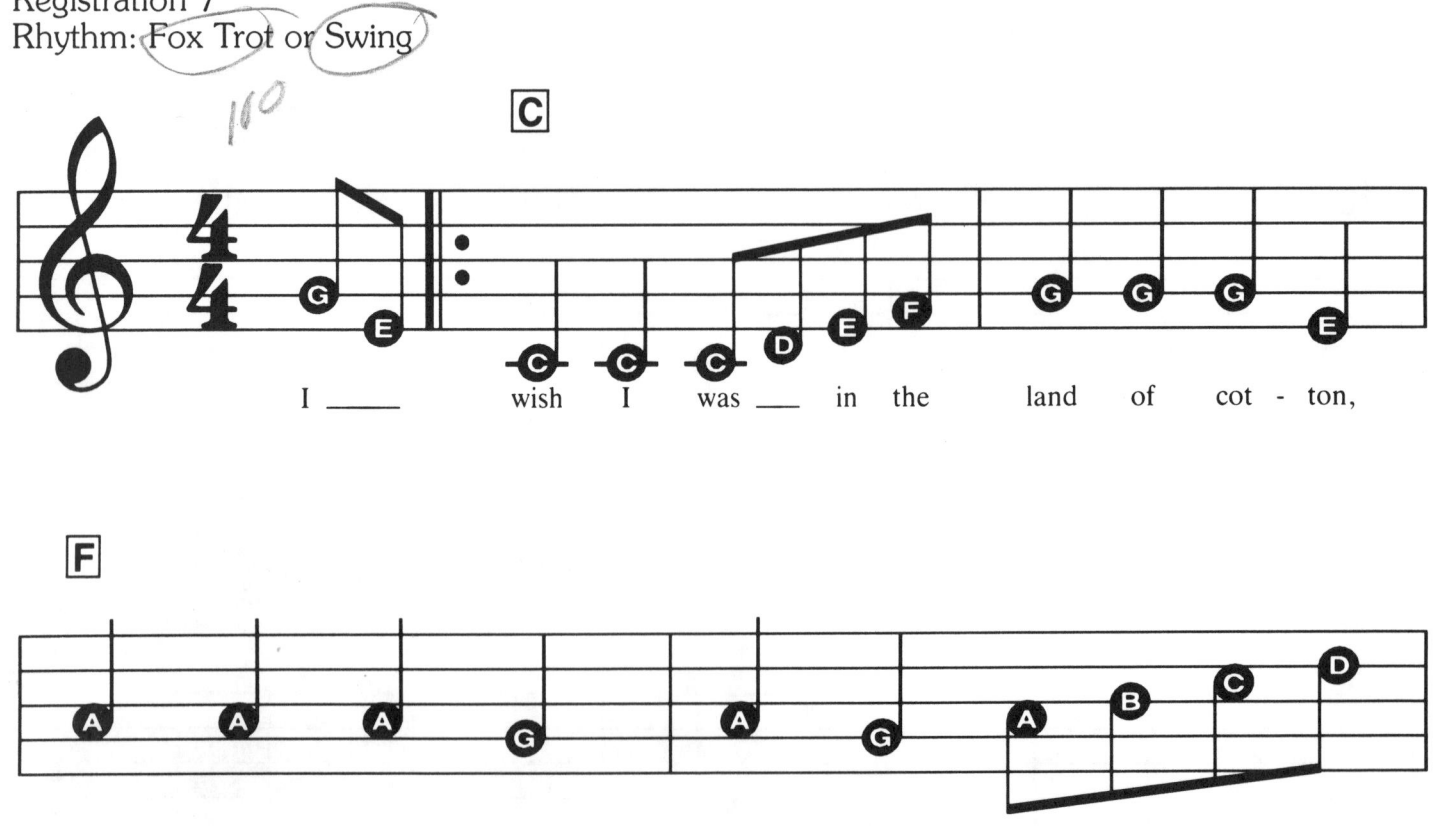

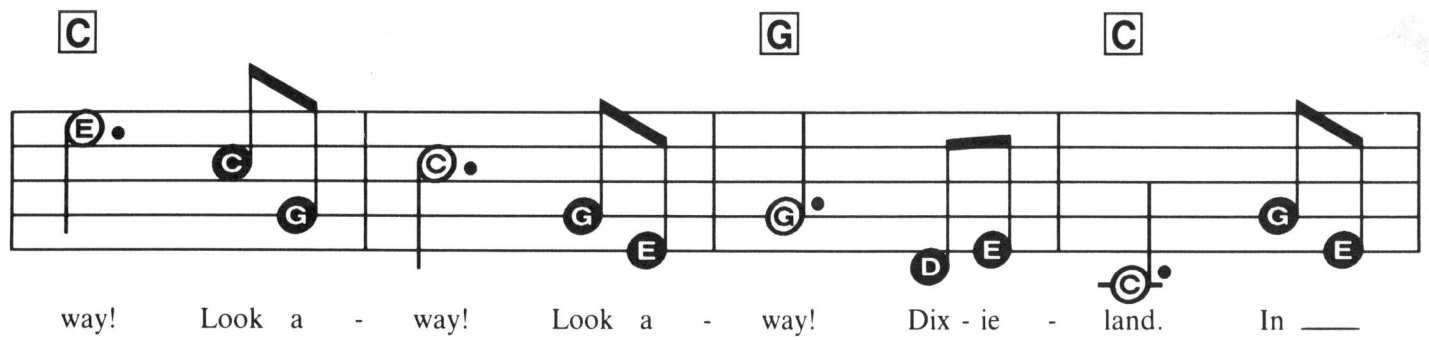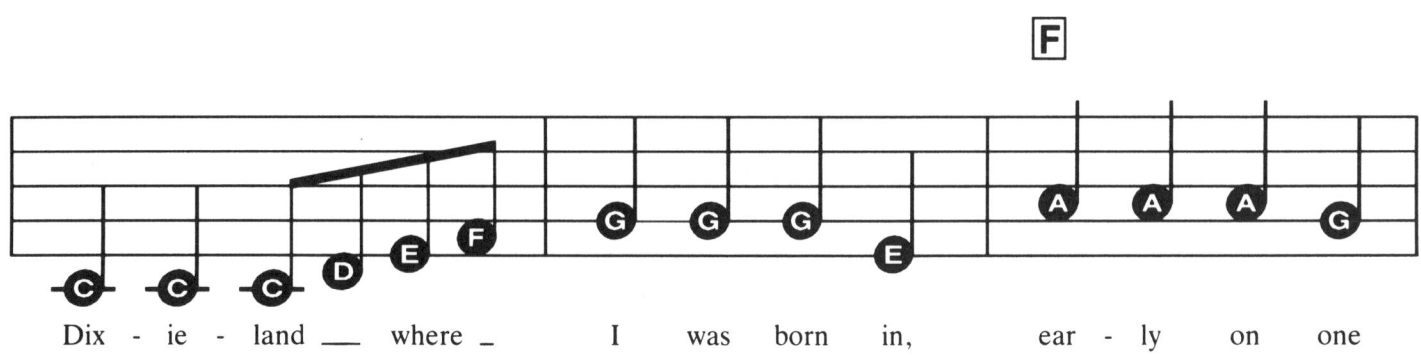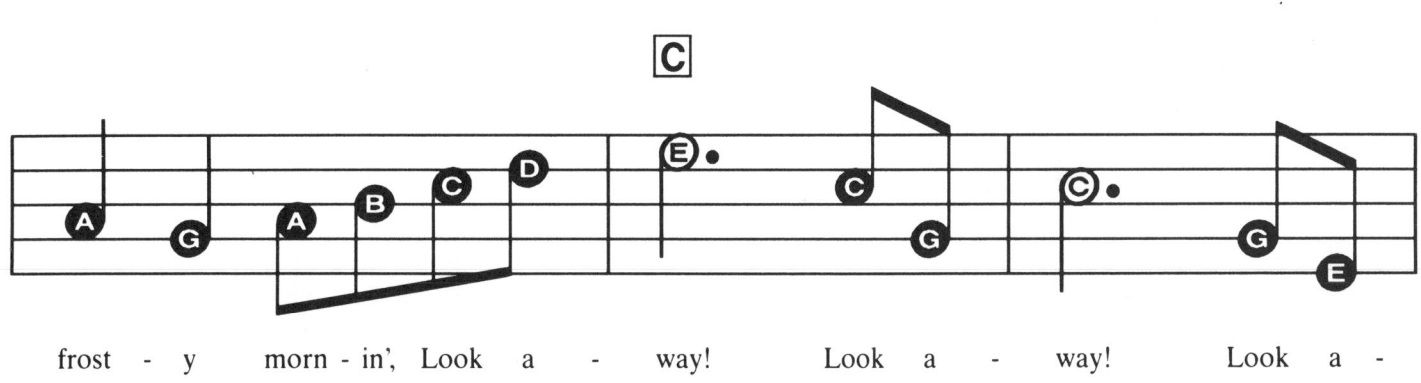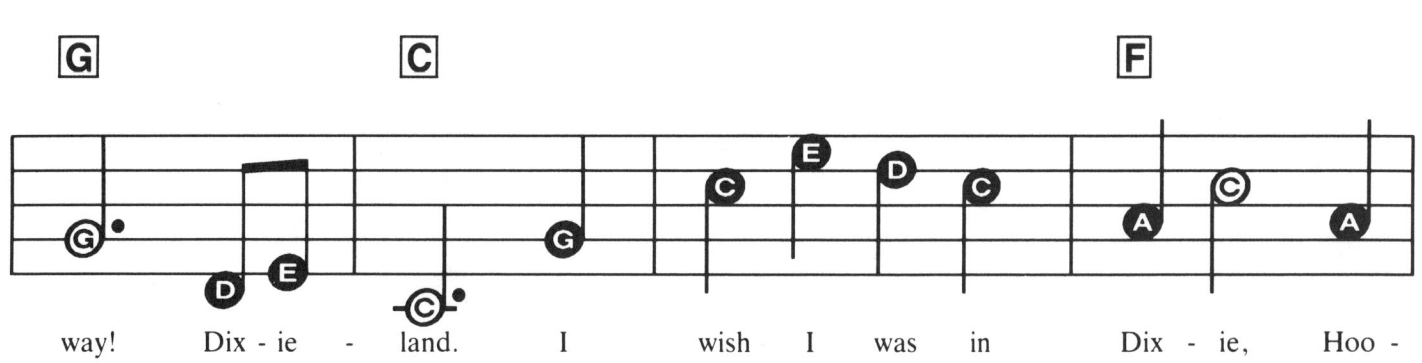

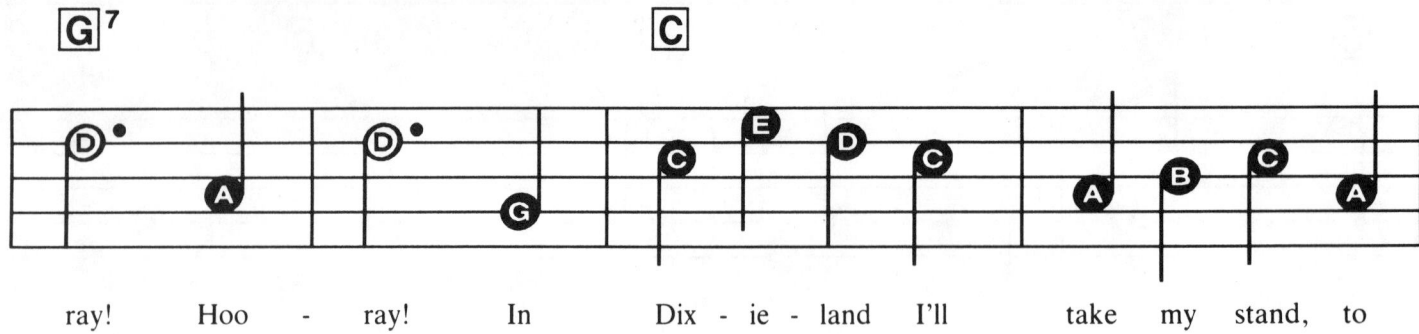
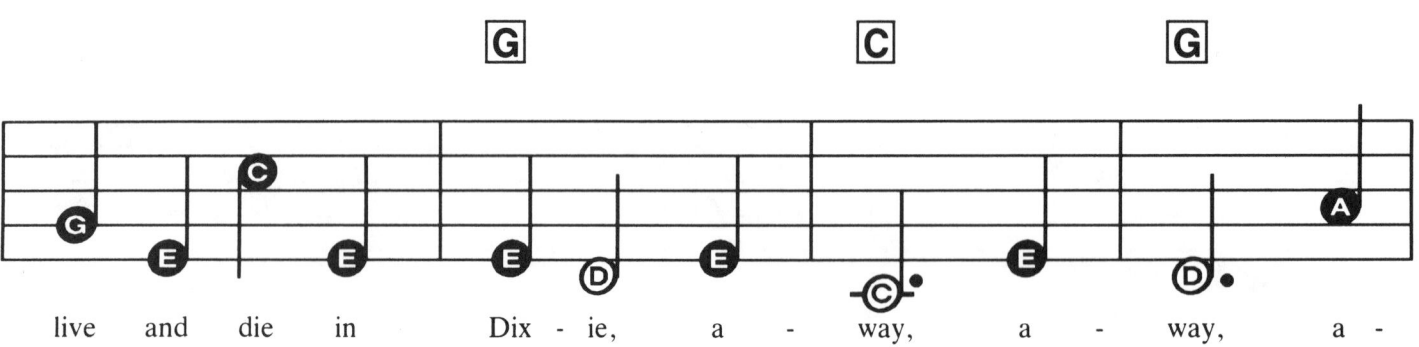
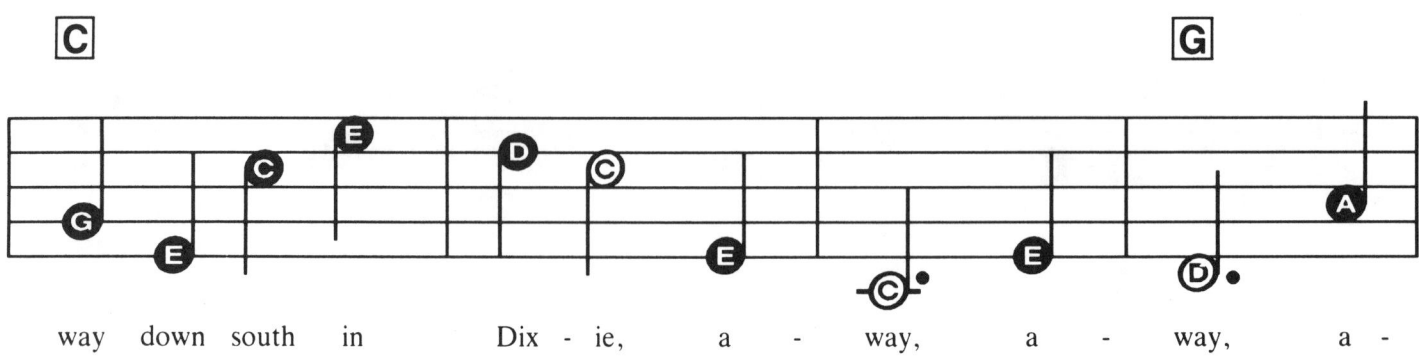
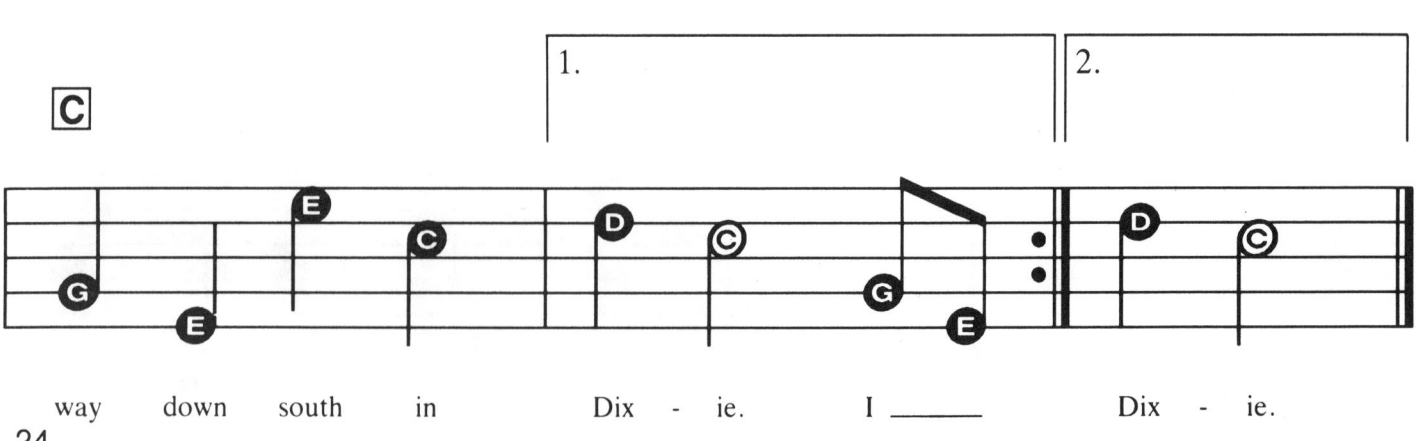

THEME FROM "THE NEW WORLD" SYMPHONY
(Going Home)

Registration 1
Rhythm: Waltz

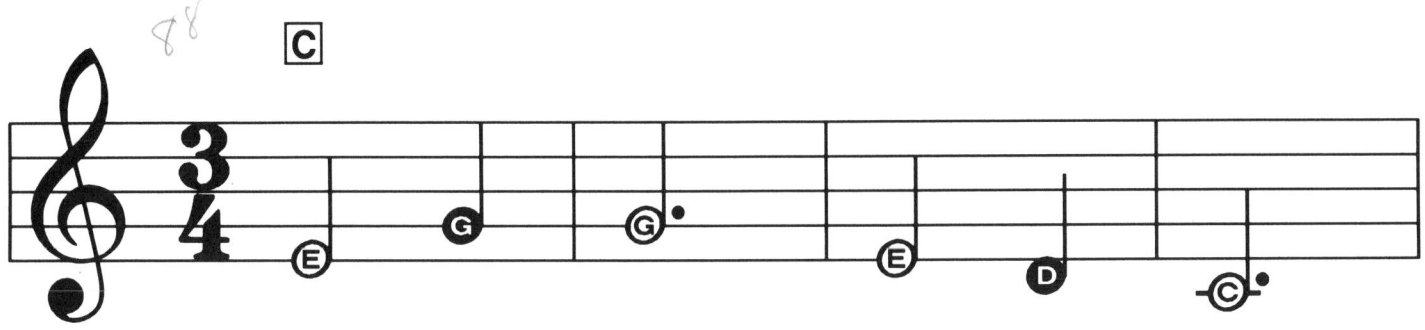
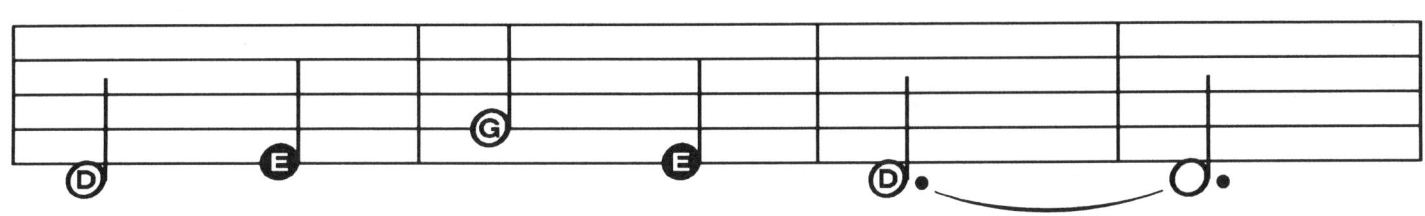
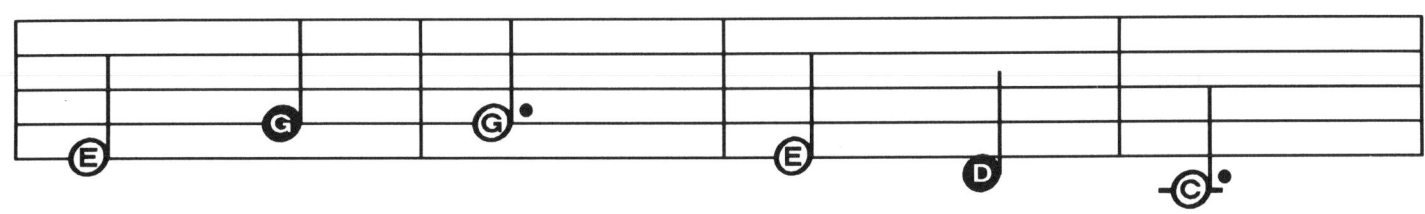
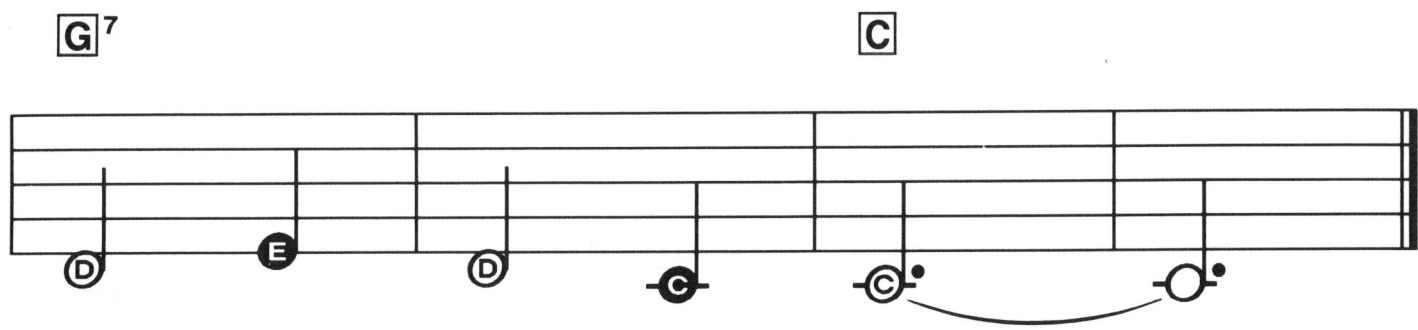

Copyright © 1972 HAL LEONARD CORPORATION
International Copyright Secured All Rights Reserved

LA SPAGNOLA

Registration 9
Rhythm: Waltz

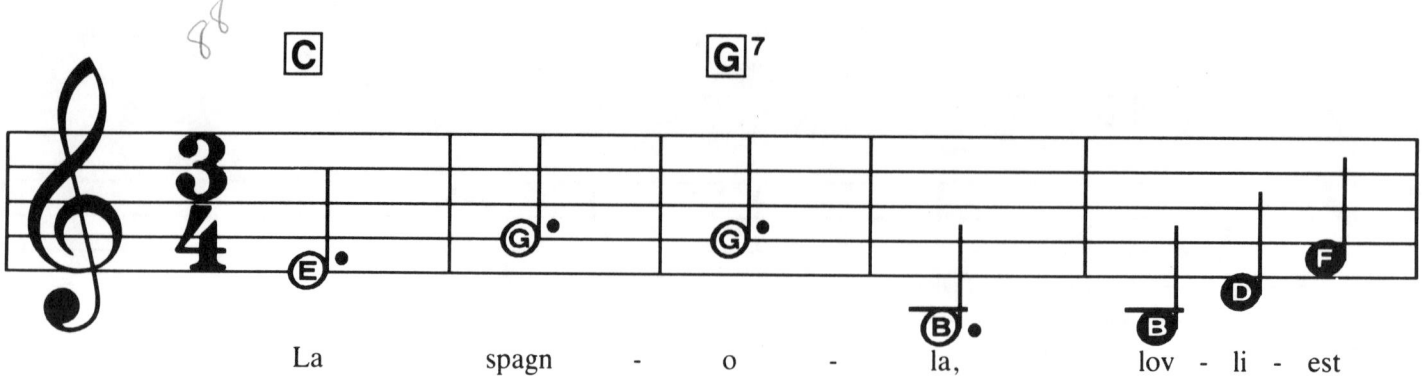
La spagn-o-la, lov-li-est

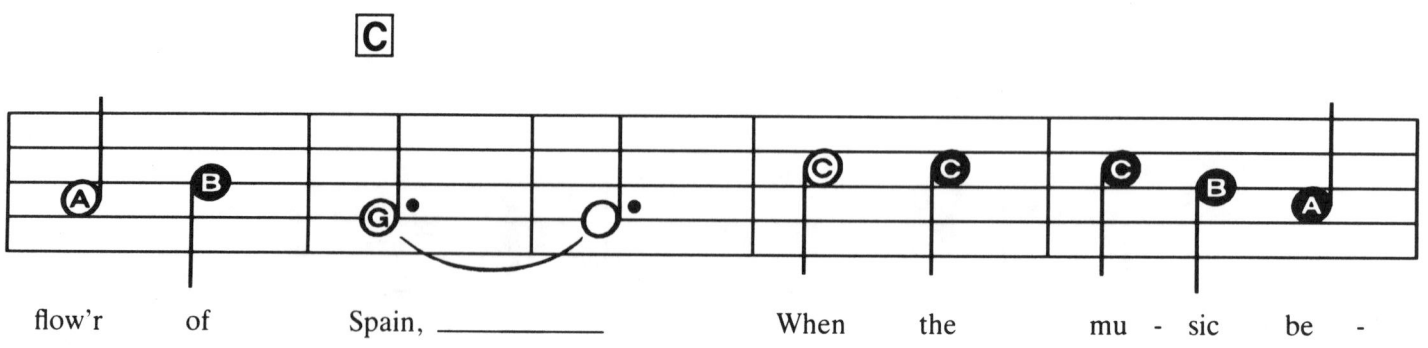
flow'r of Spain, When the mu-sic be-

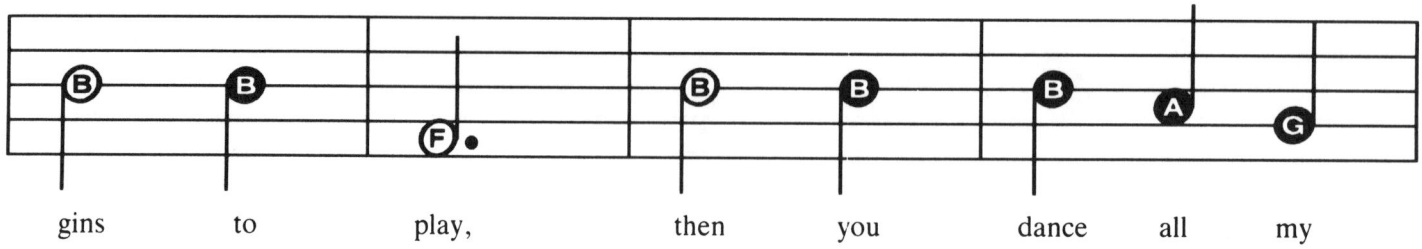
gins to play, then you dance all my

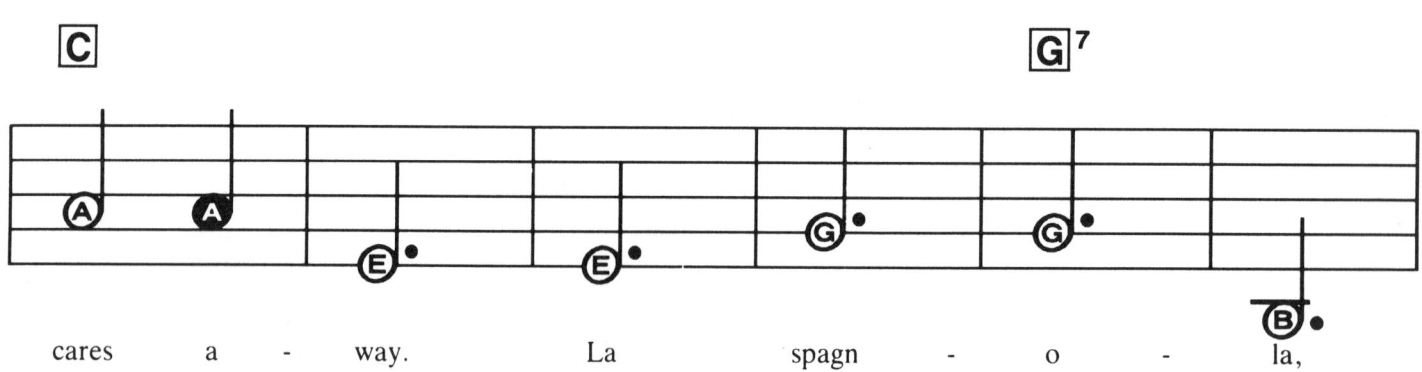
cares a-way. La spagn-o-la,

Copyright © 1972 HAL LEONARD CORPORATION
International Copyright Secured   All Rights Reserved

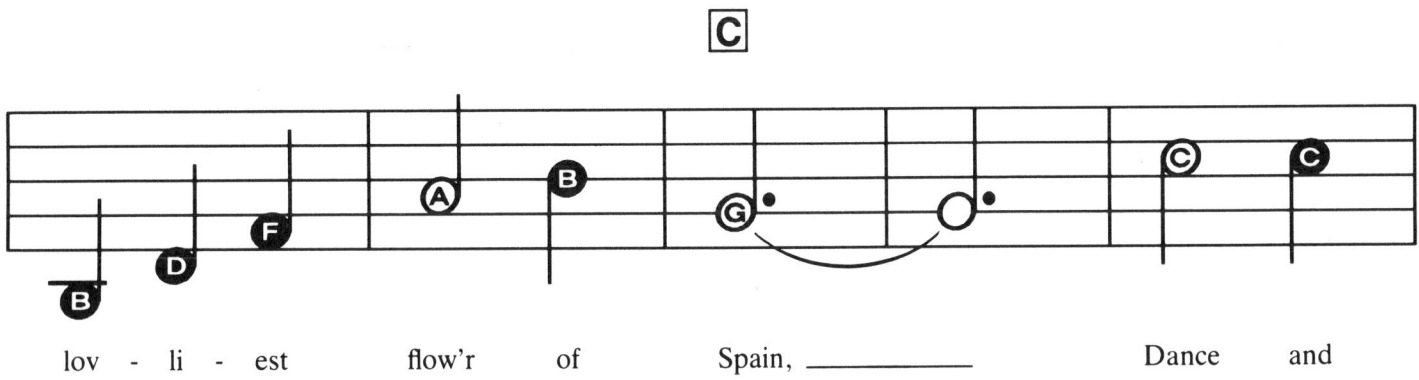
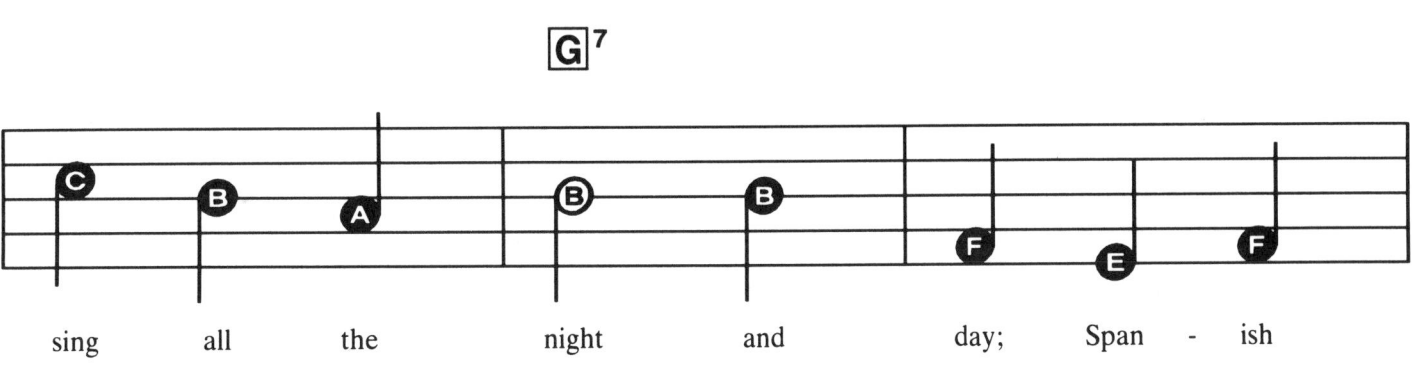
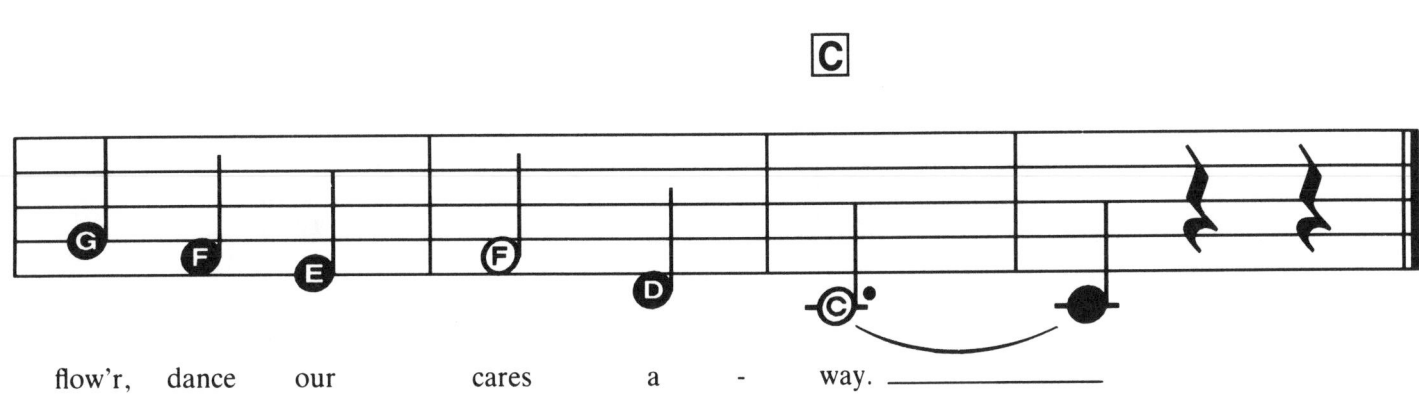

MAORI FAREWELL SONG

Registration 7
Rhythm: Waltz

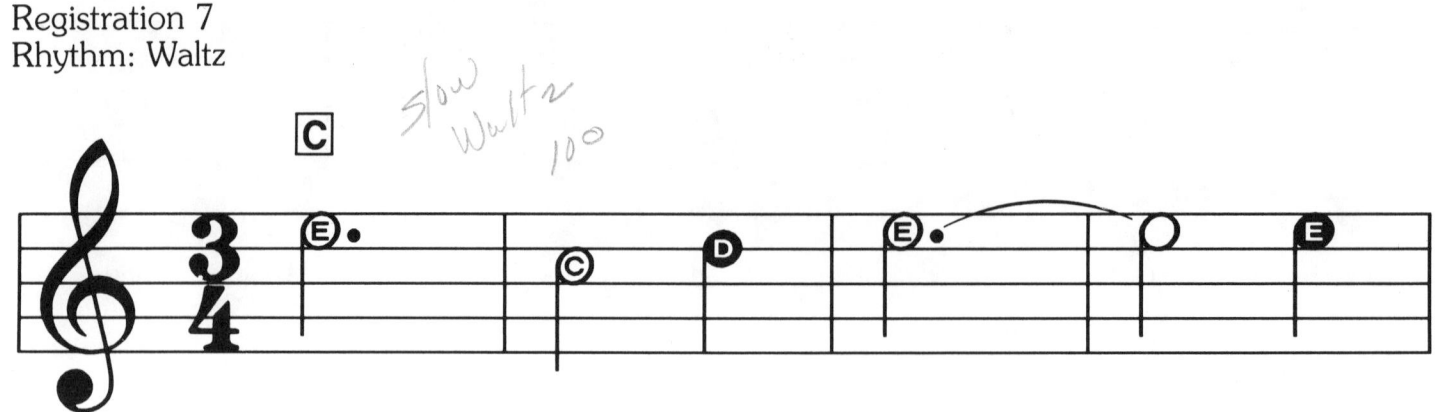
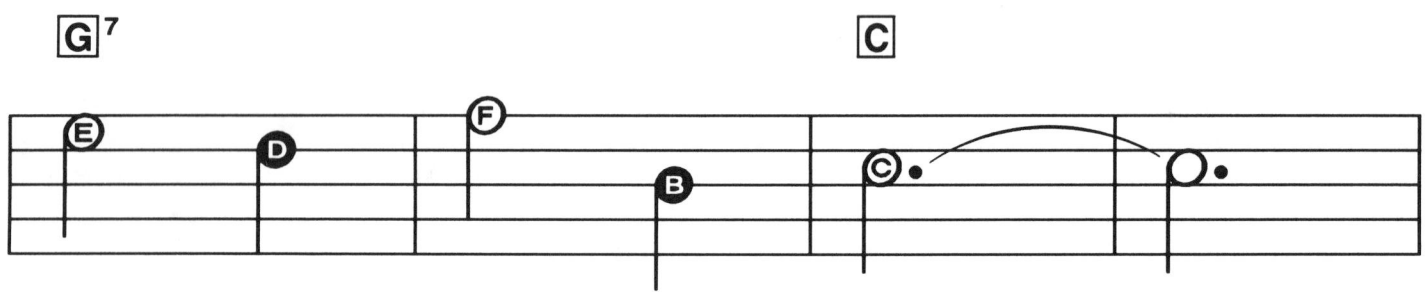
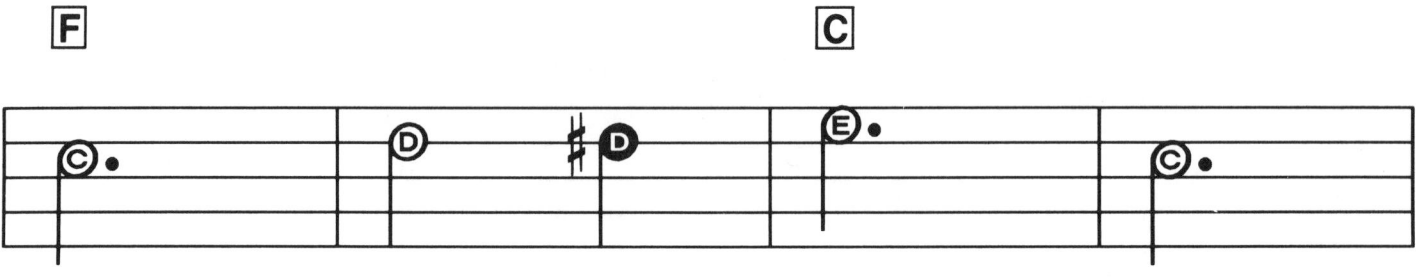
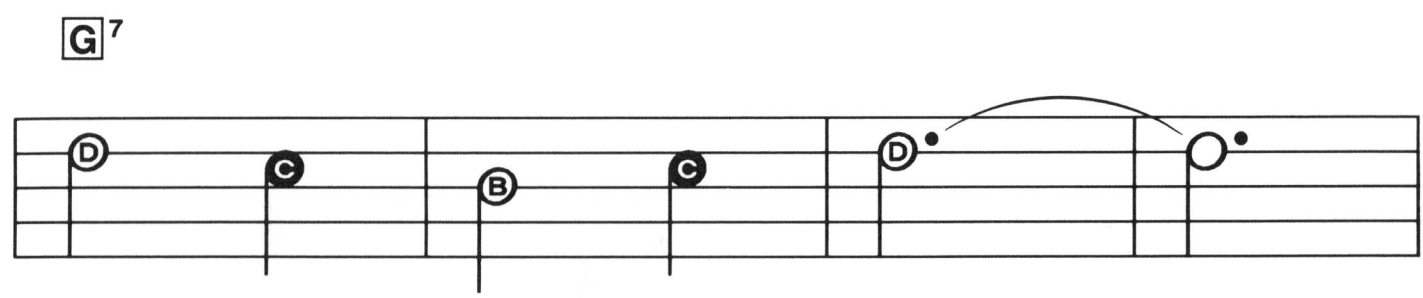

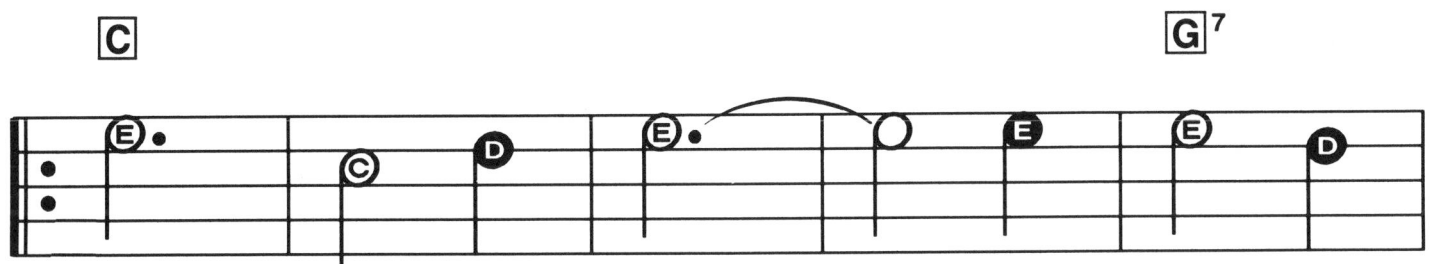
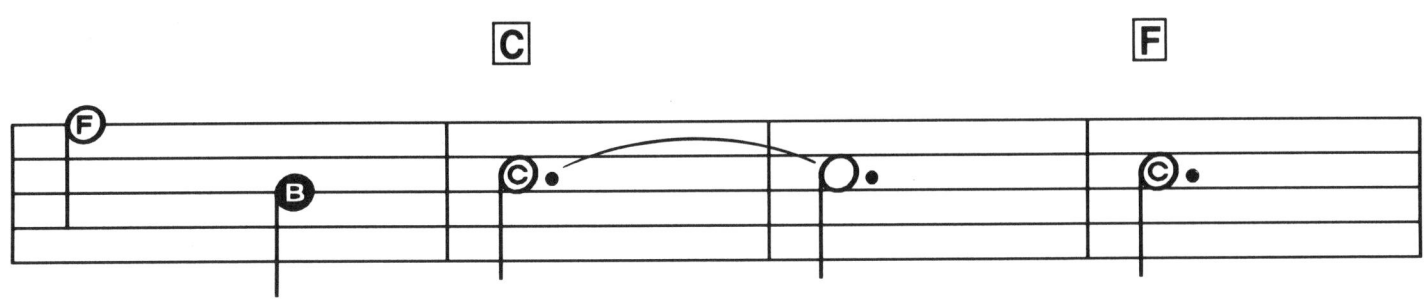
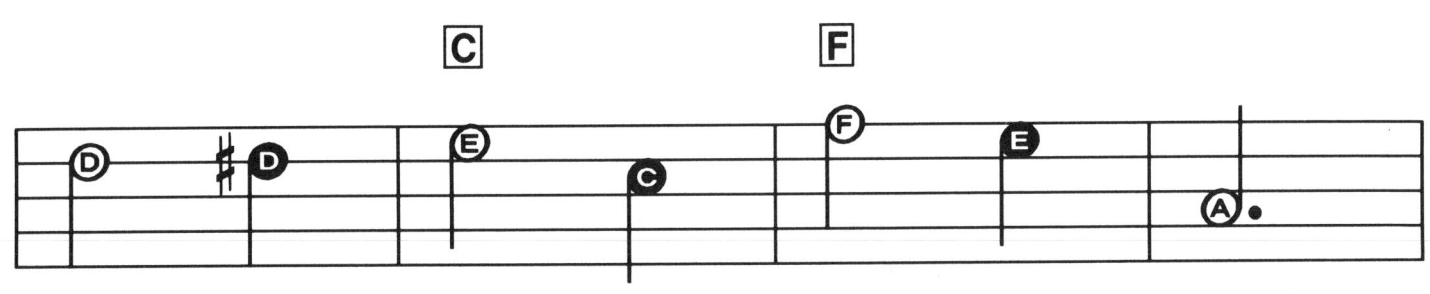
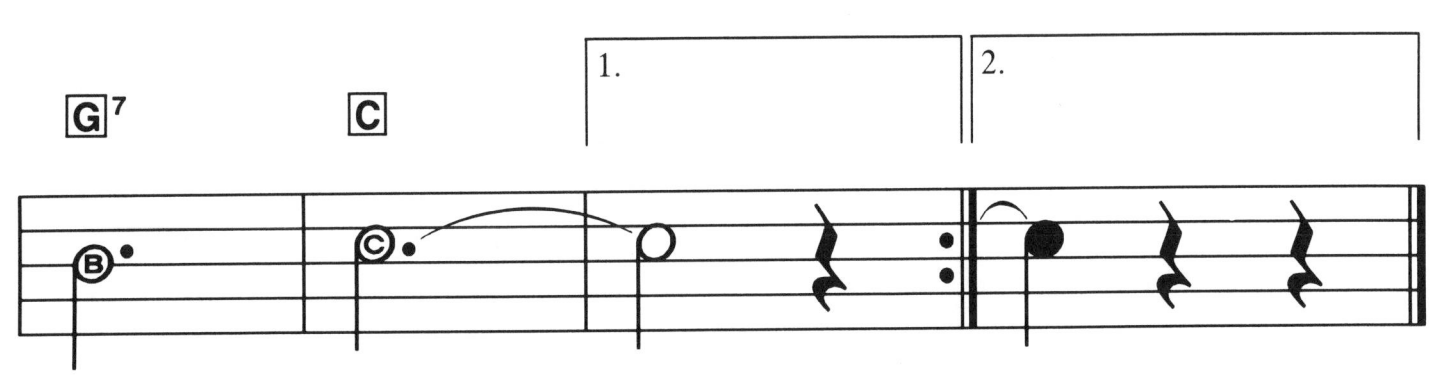

29

SANTA LUCIA

Registration 10
Rhythm: Waltz

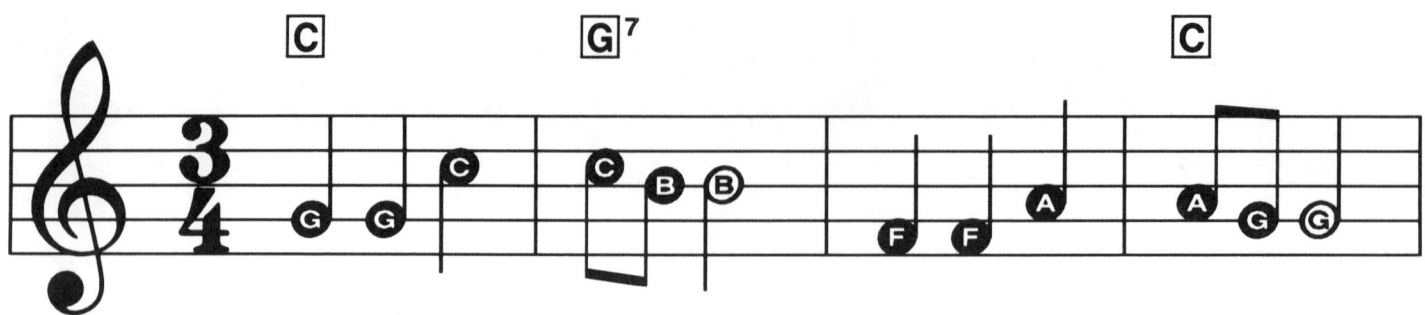
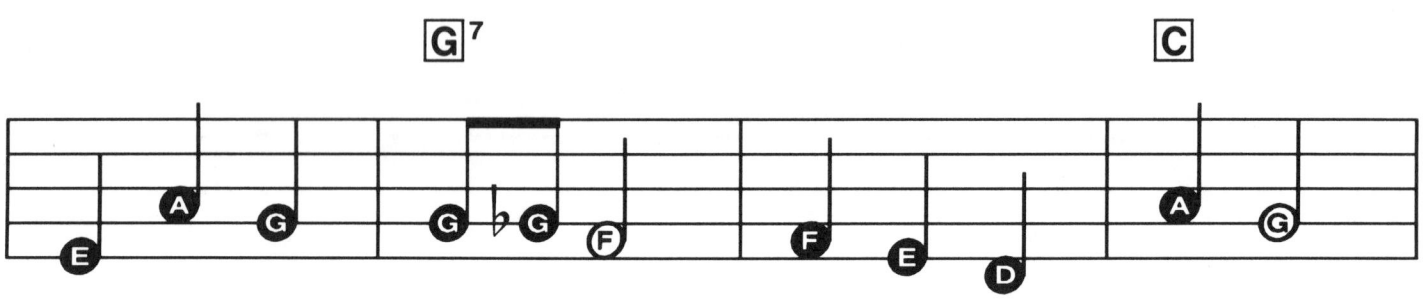
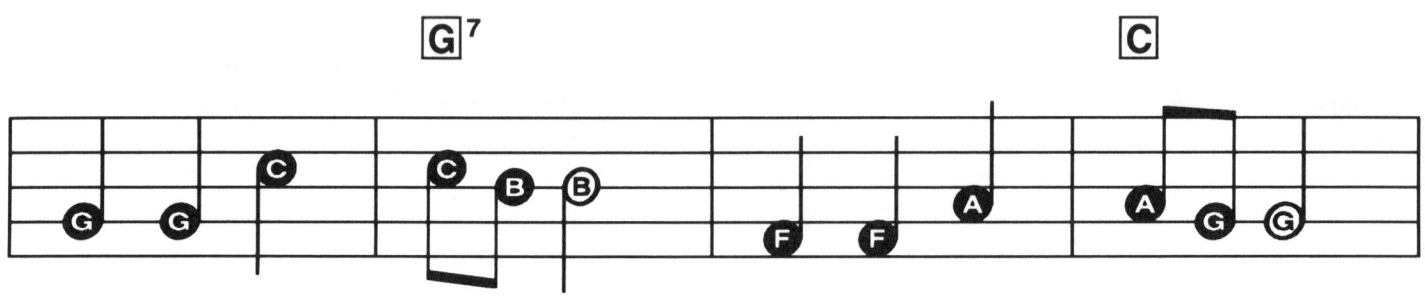
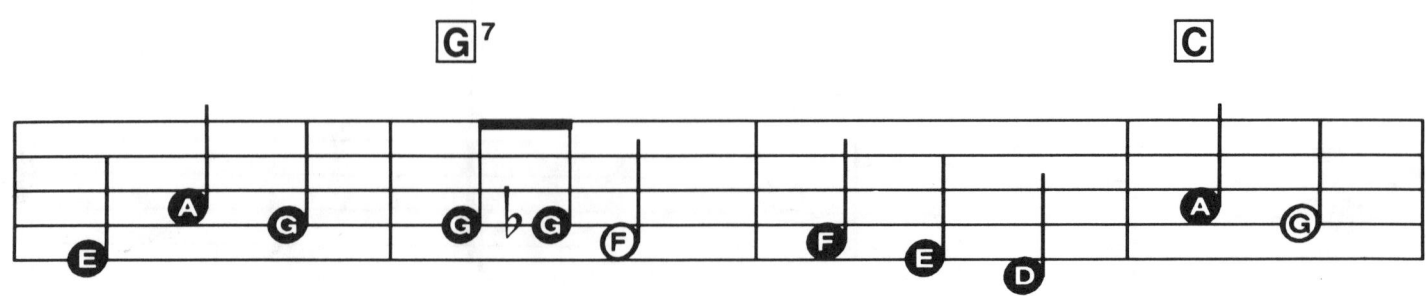

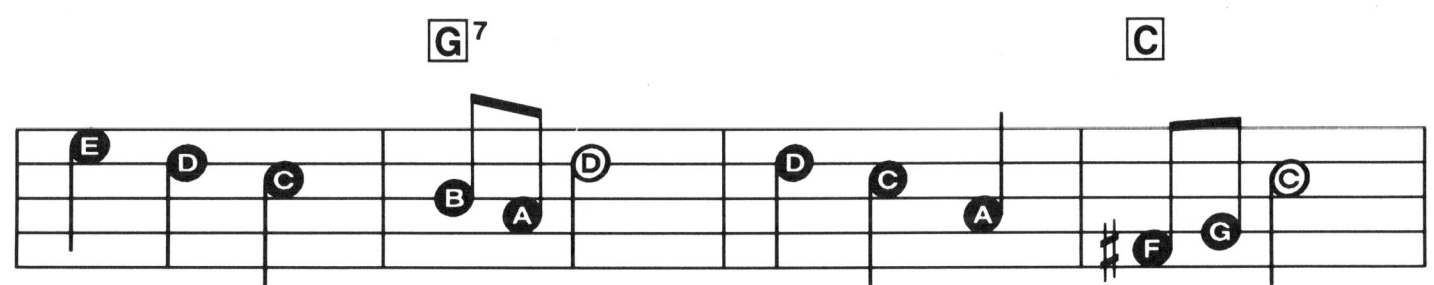
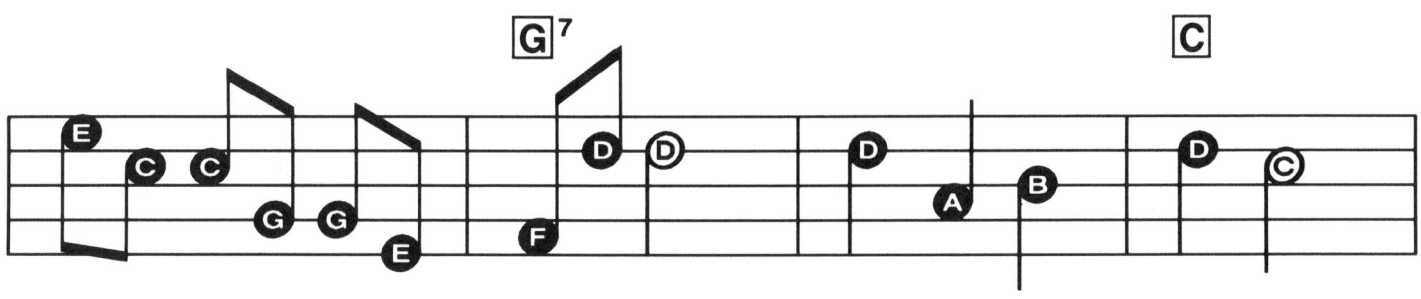
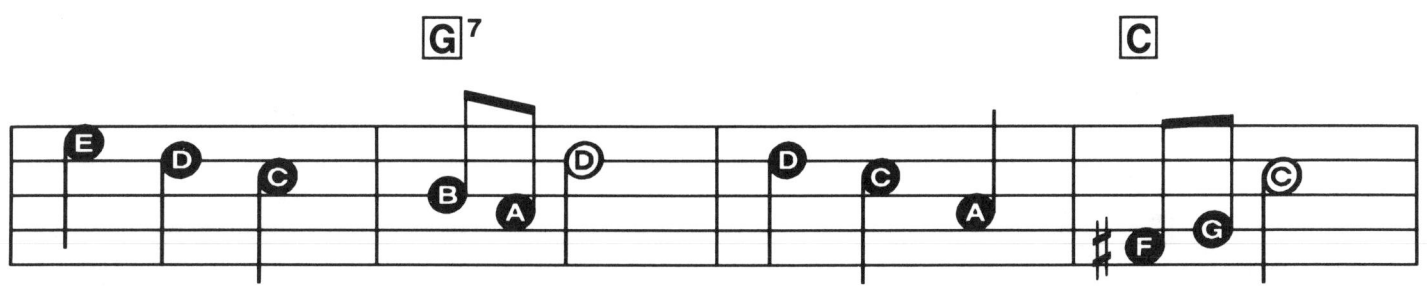
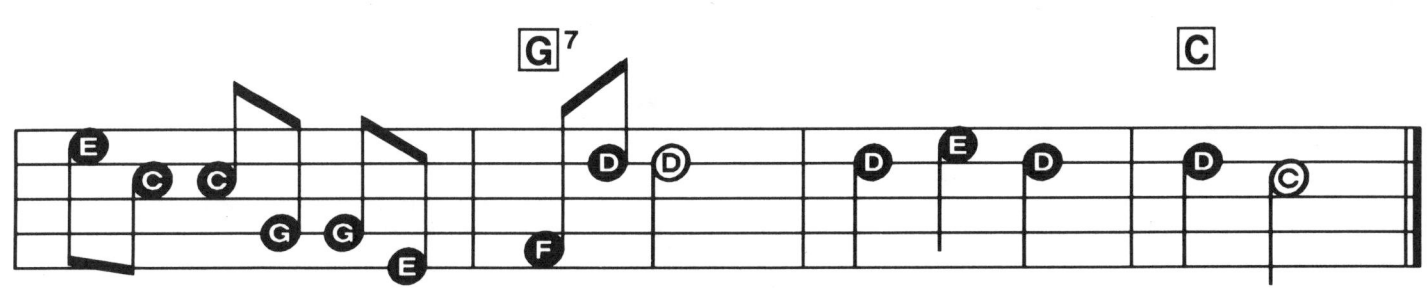

SWANEE RIVER

Registration 2
Rhythm: Fox Trot or Swing

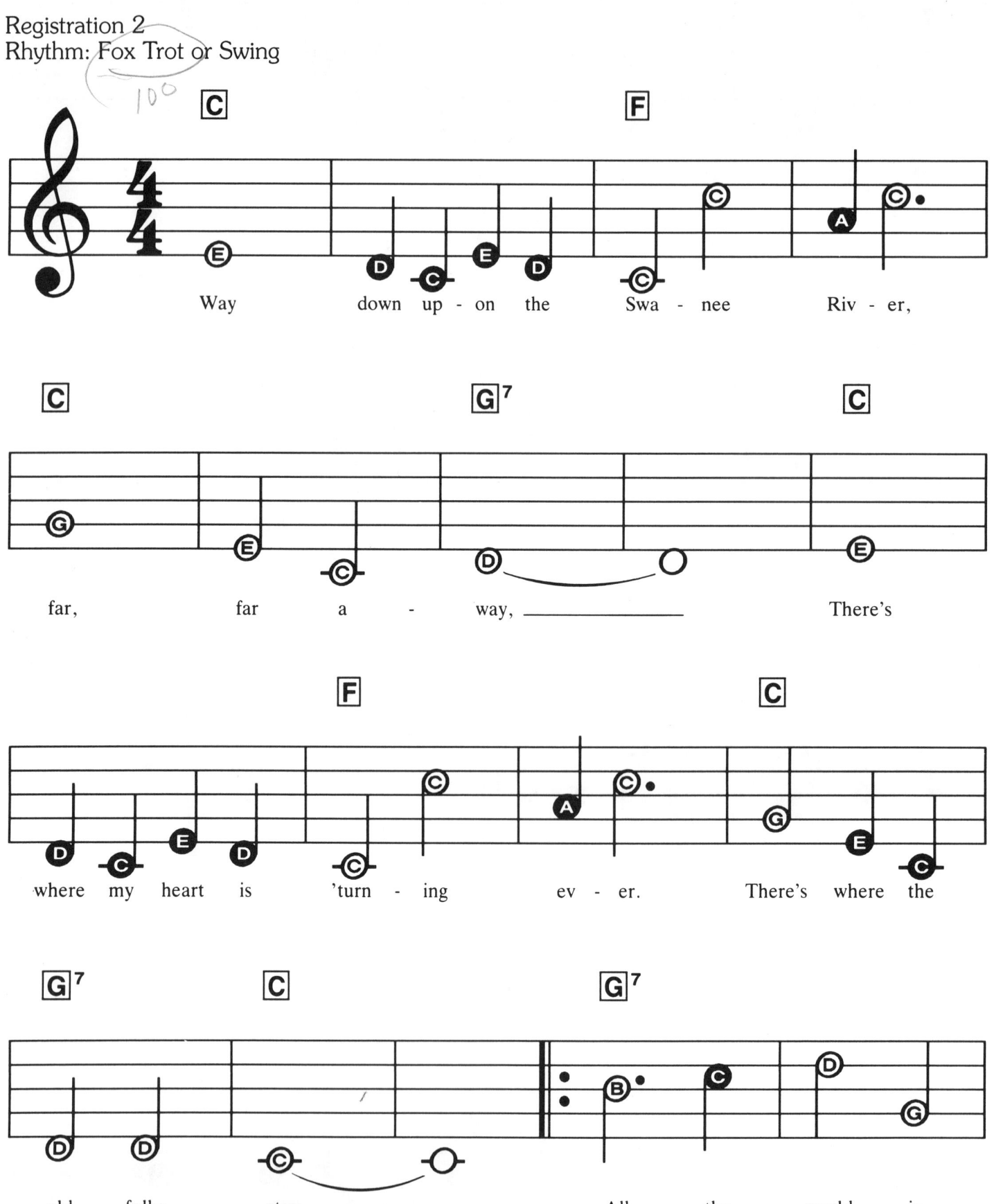

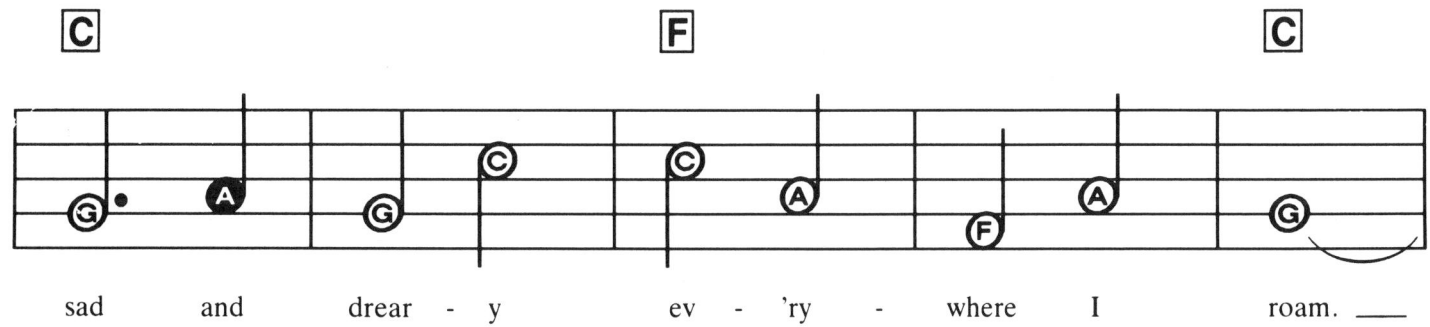
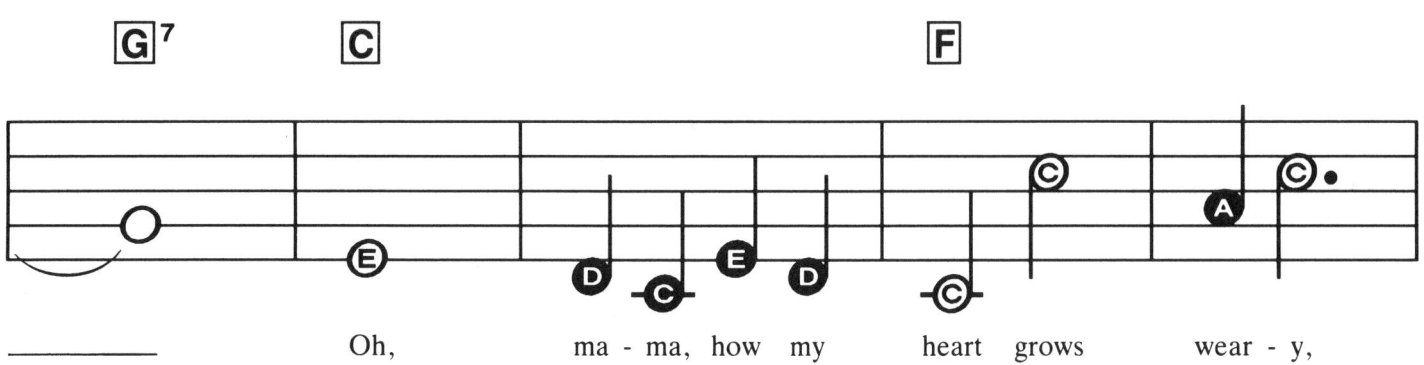
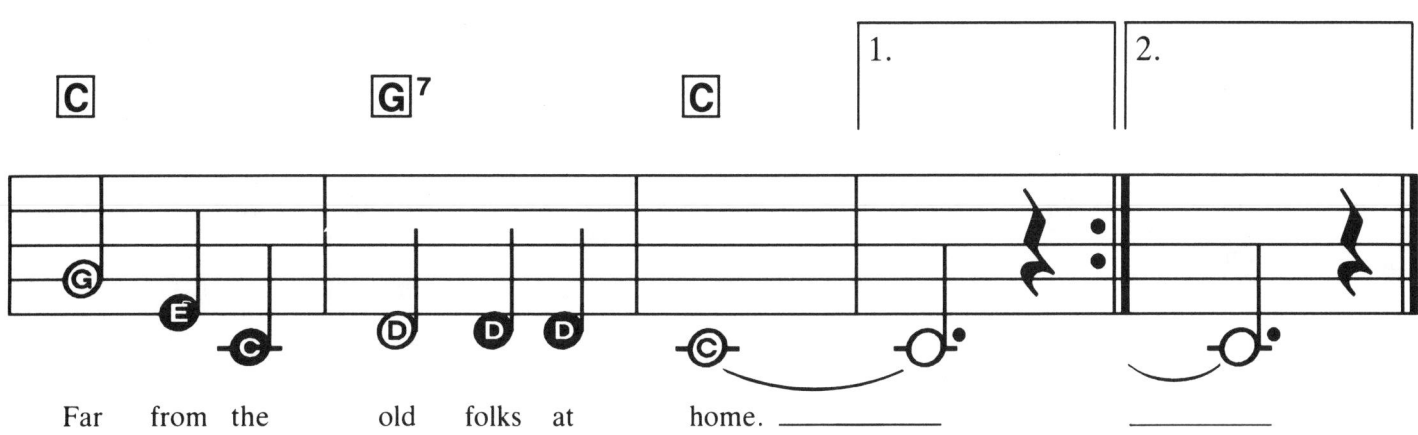

WHEN THE SAINTS GO MARCHING IN

Registration 7
Rhythm: Swing

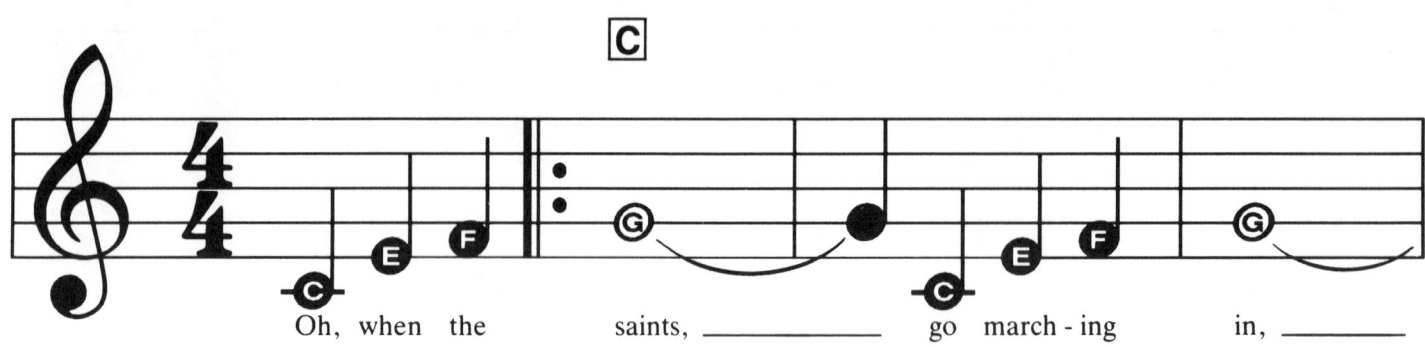

BEAUTIFUL BROWN EYES

Registration 4
Rhythm: Waltz

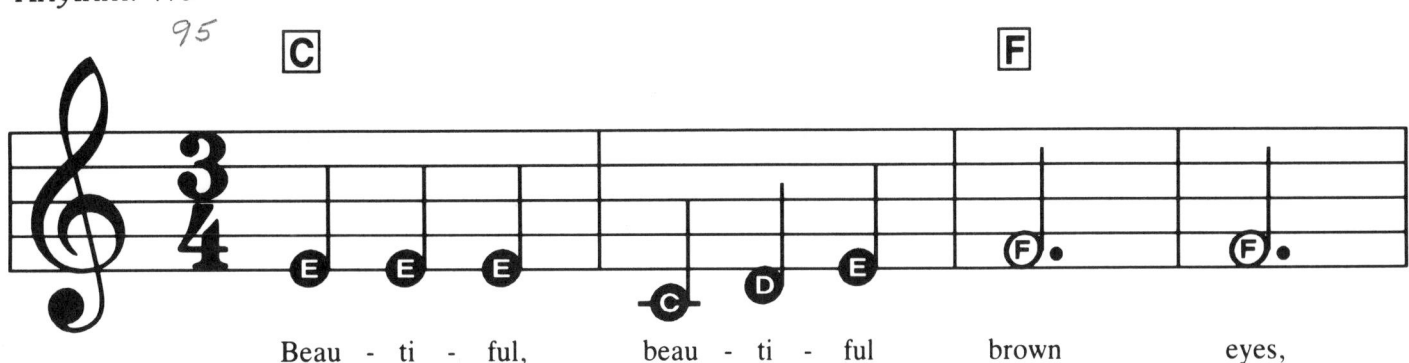

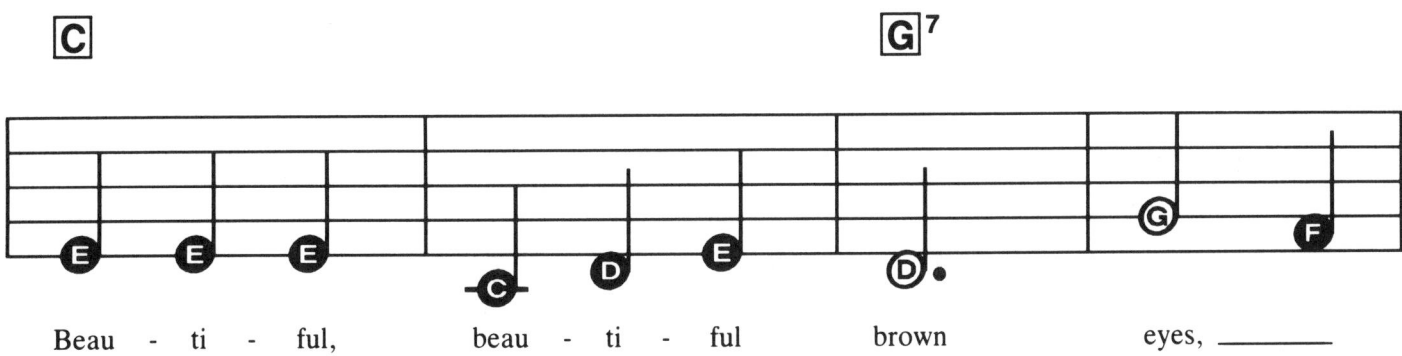

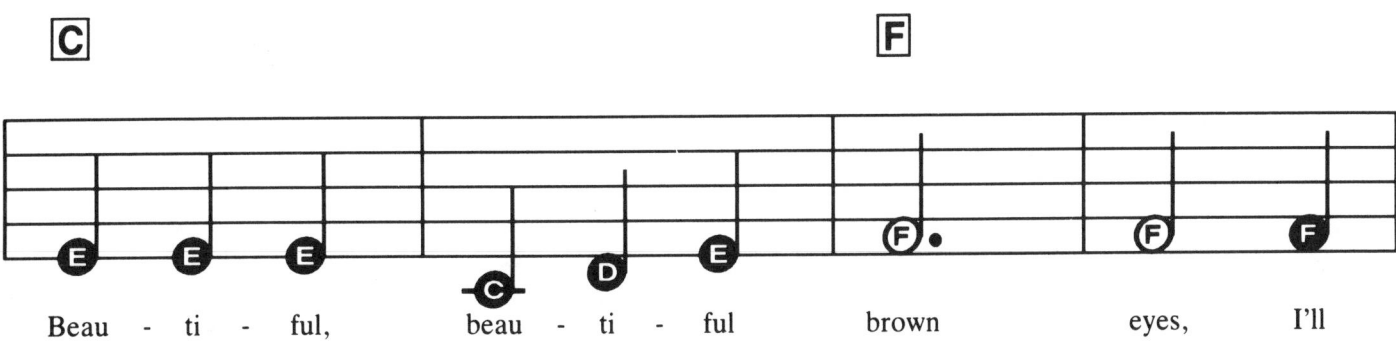

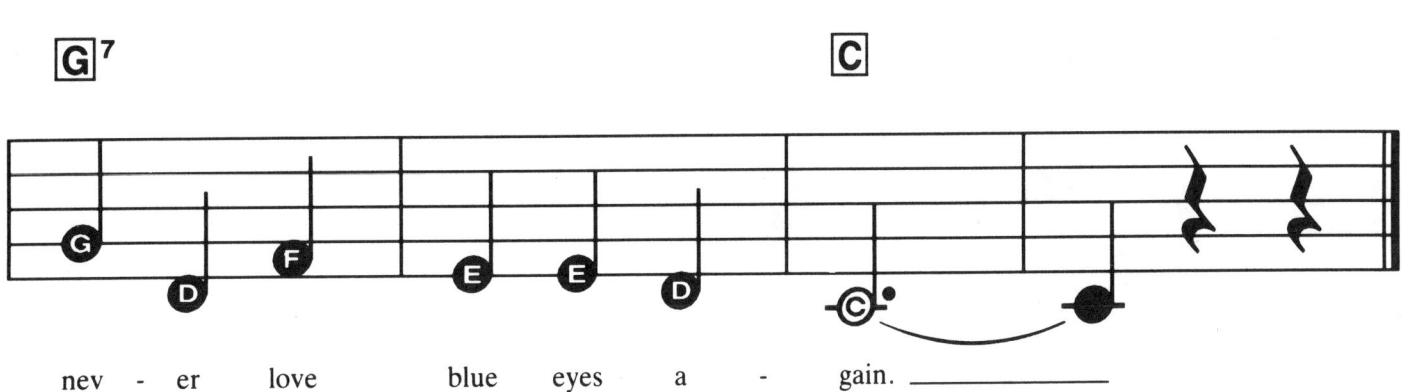

DOWN IN THE VALLEY

Registration 1
Rhythm: Waltz

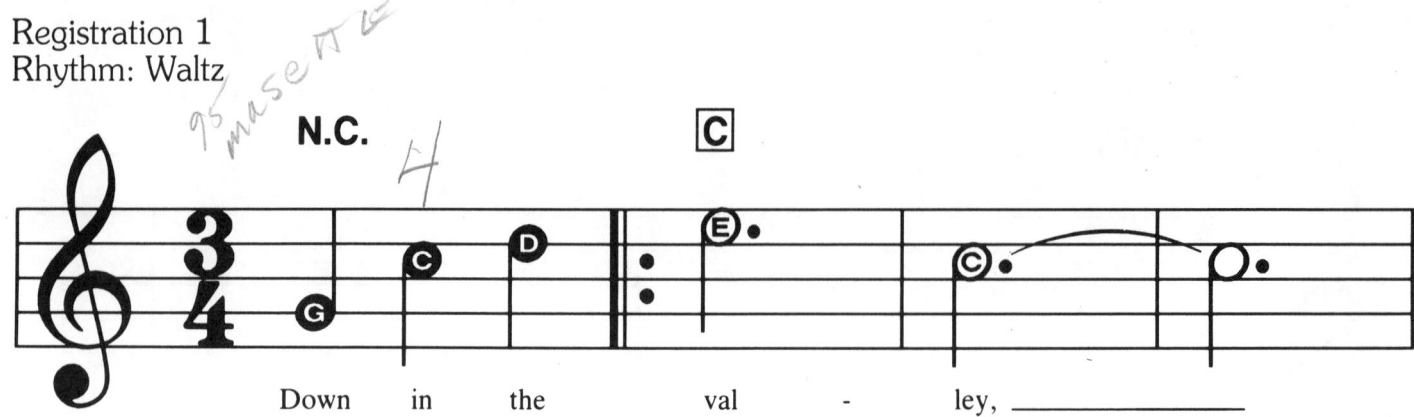

Down in the val - ley,

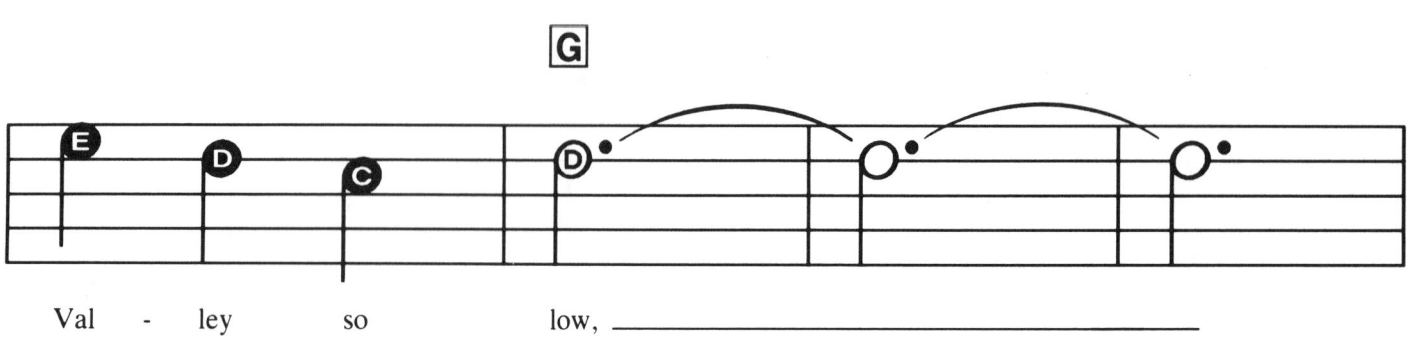

Val - ley so low,

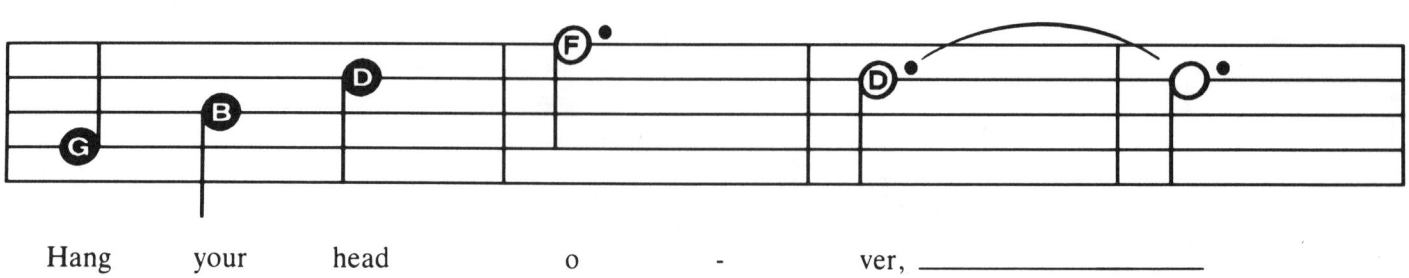

Hang your head o - ver,

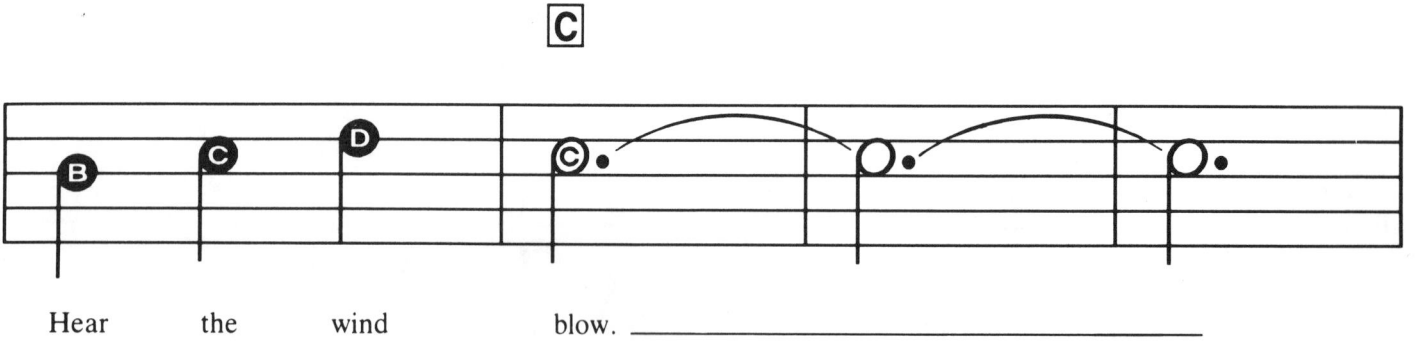

Hear the wind blow.

Hear the wind blow, boys,

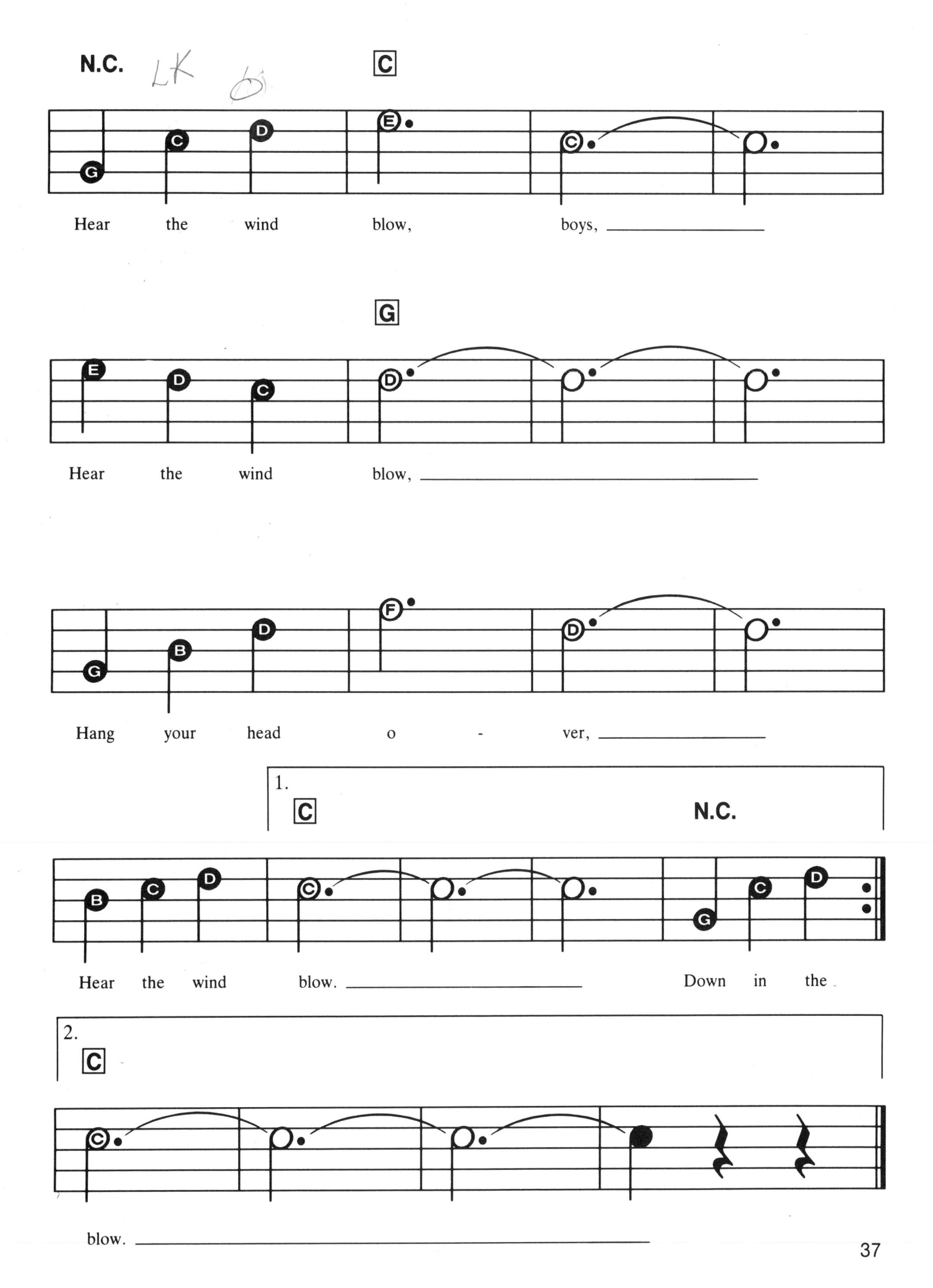

Hear the wind blow,

Hang your head o - ver,

1.
Hear the wind blow. Down in the

2.
blow.

37

MELODY OF LOVE

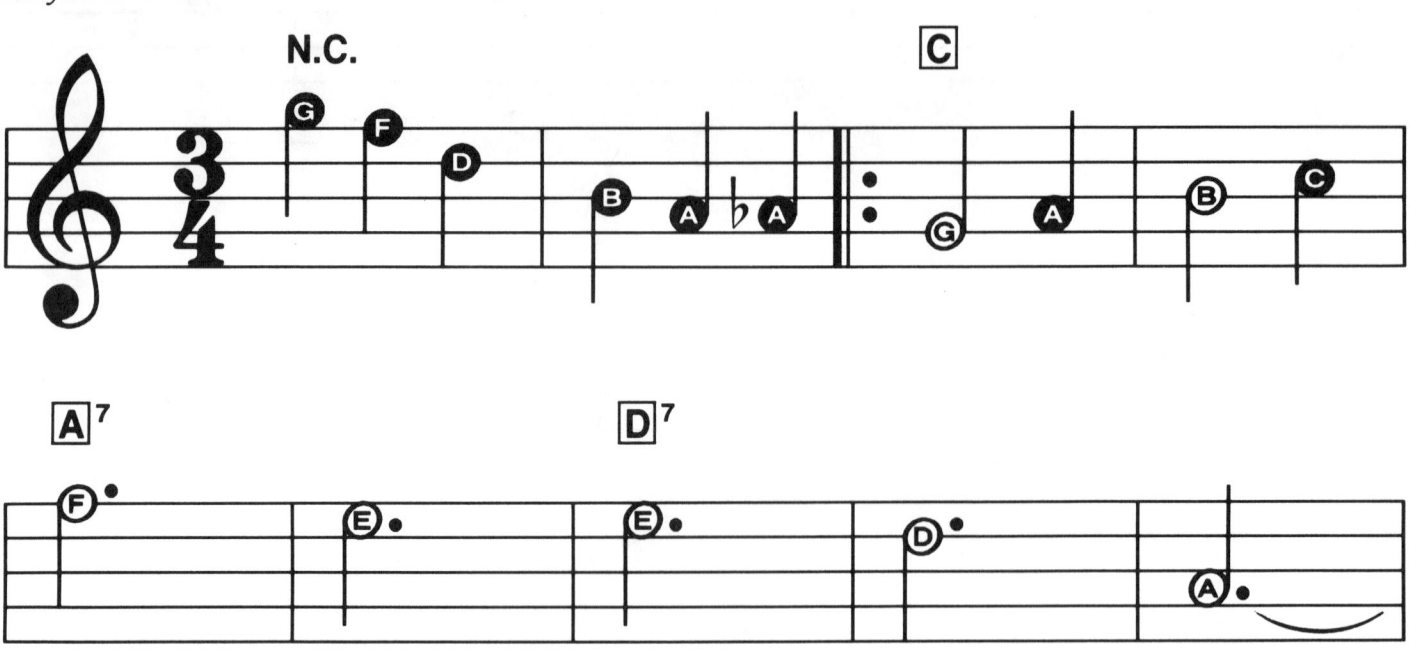

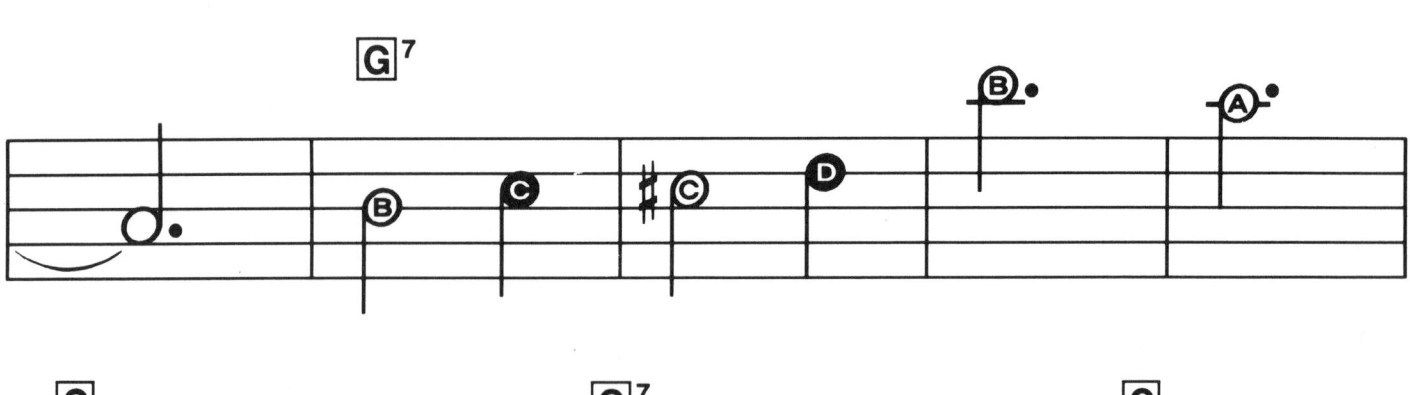

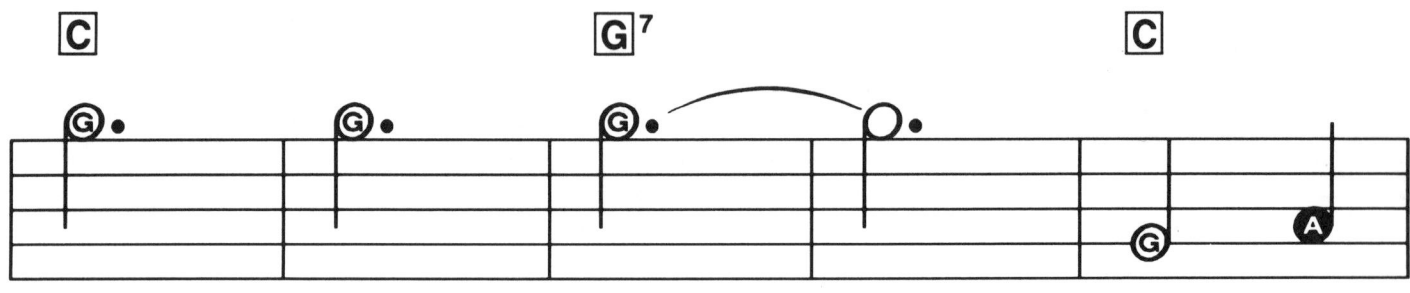

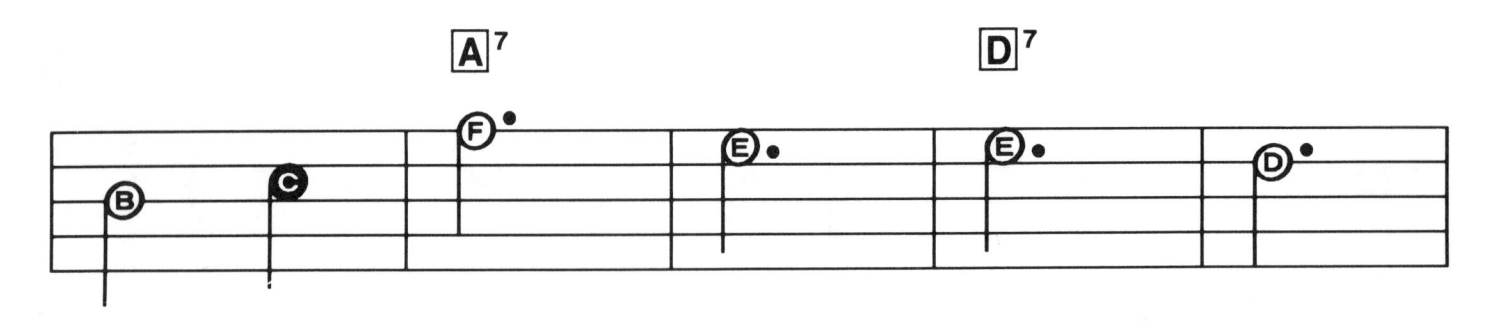

Registration 9
Rhythm: Waltz

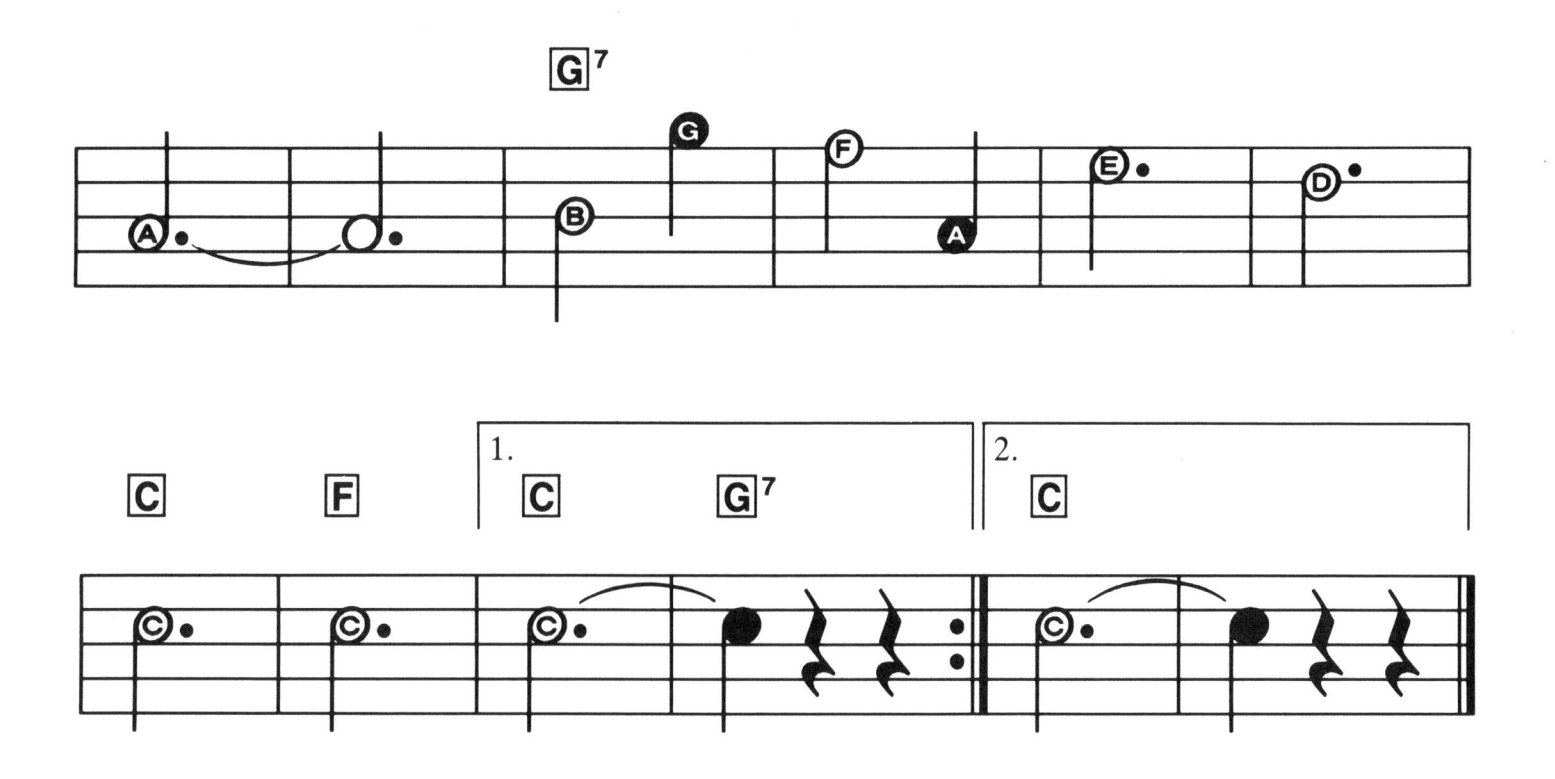

LITTLE BROWN JUG

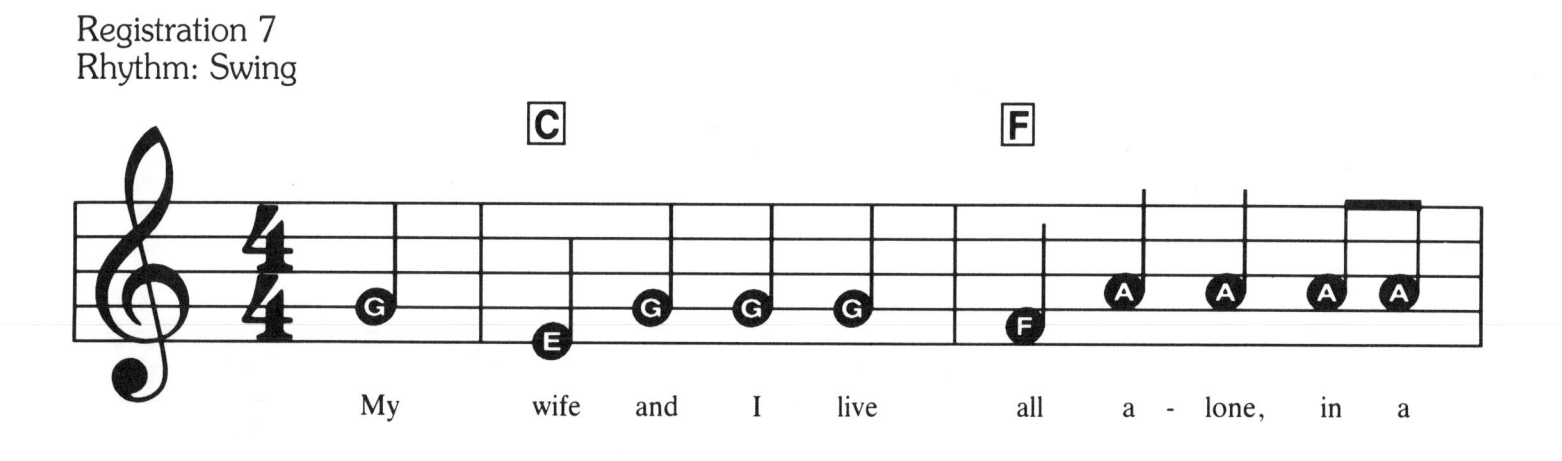

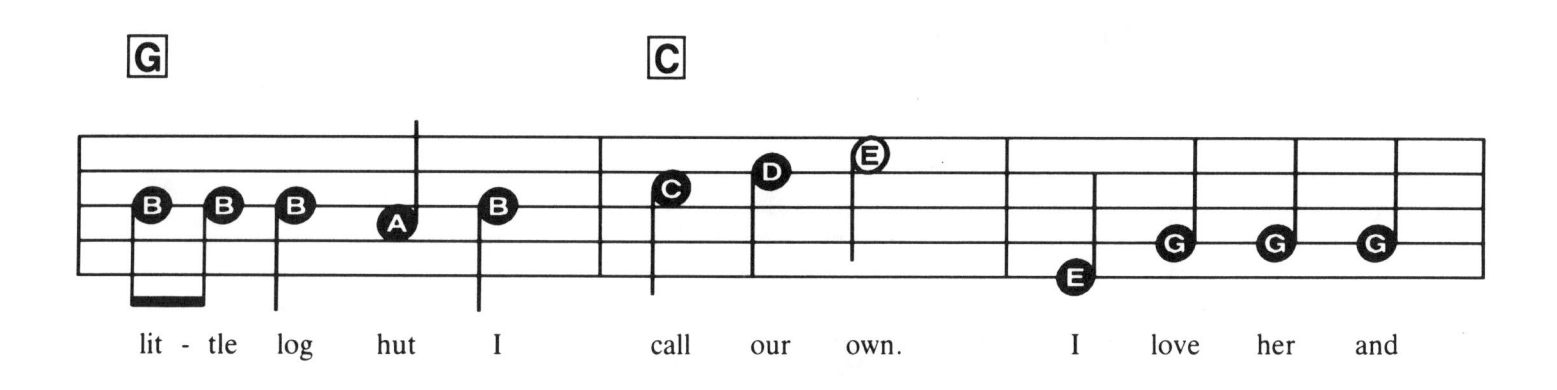

Registration 7
Rhythm: Swing

My wife and I live all a-lone, in a little log hut I call our own. I love her and

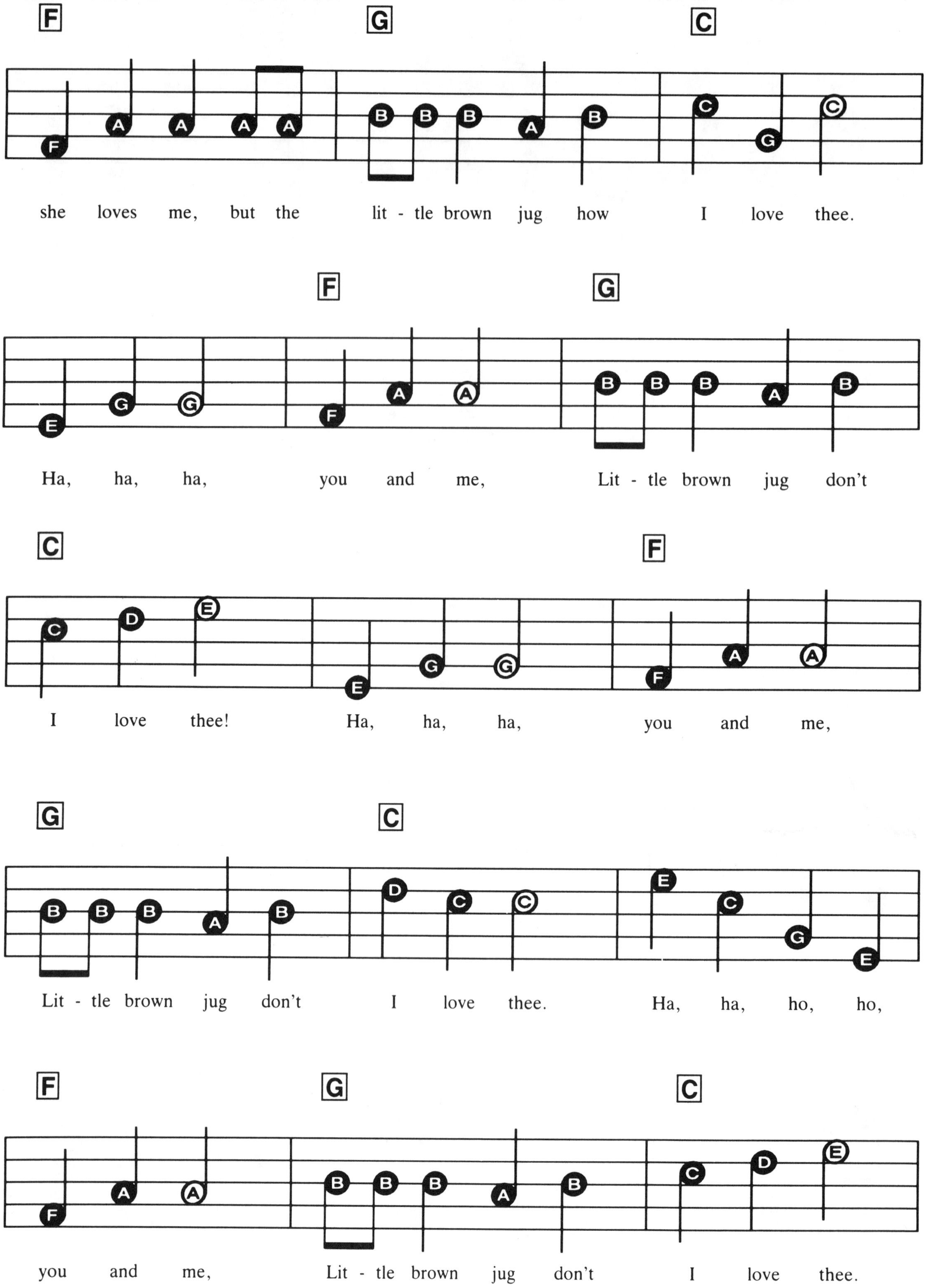
F G C
she loves me, but the lit - tle brown jug how I love thee.
F G
Ha, ha, ha, you and me, Lit - tle brown jug don't
C F
I love thee! Ha, ha, ha, you and me,
G C
Lit - tle brown jug don't I love thee. Ha, ha, ho, ho,
F G C
you and me, Lit - tle brown jug don't I love thee.

41

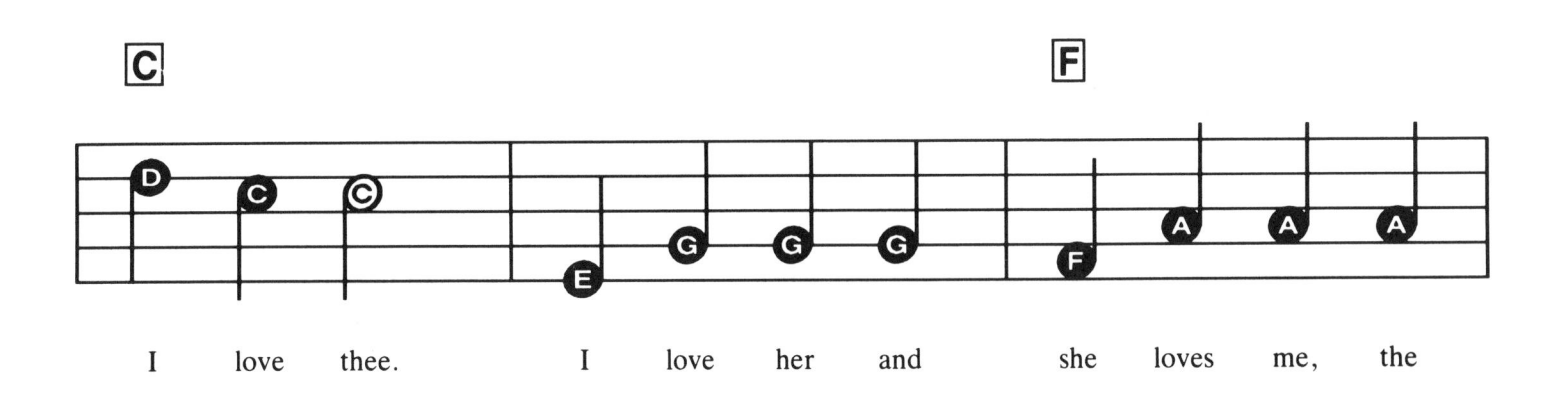

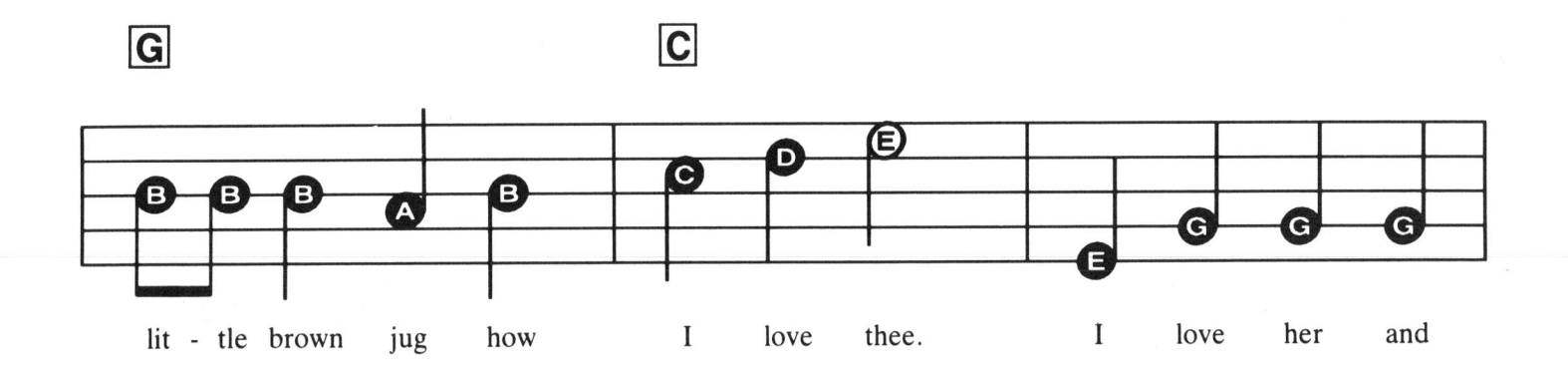

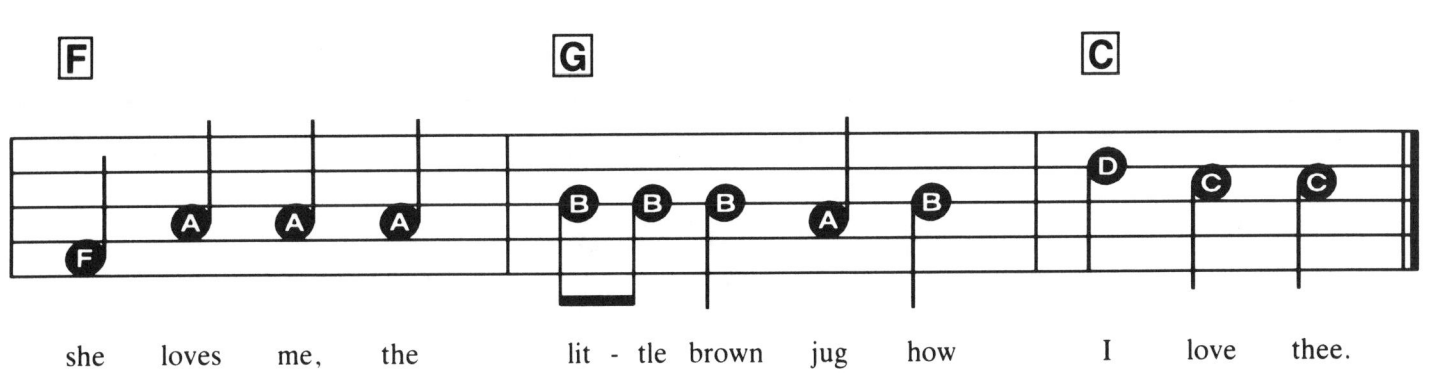

THE SKATER'S WALTZ

Registration 2
Rhythm: Waltz

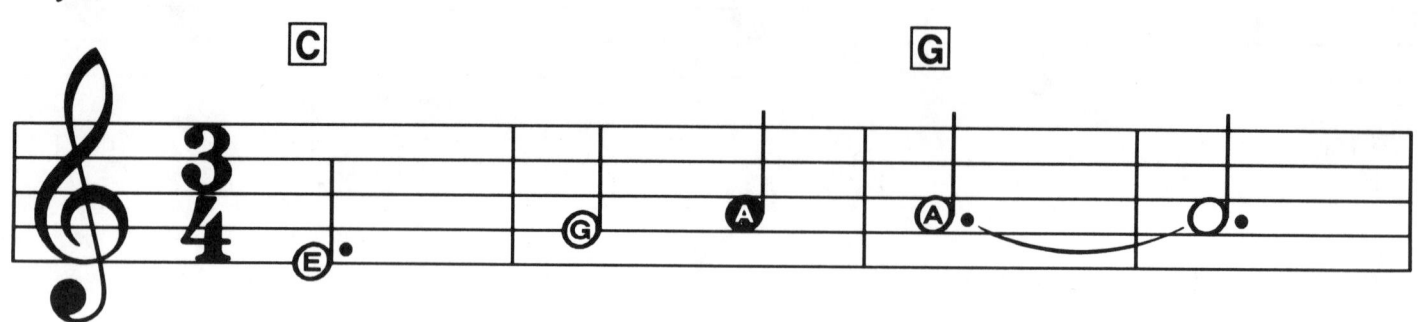

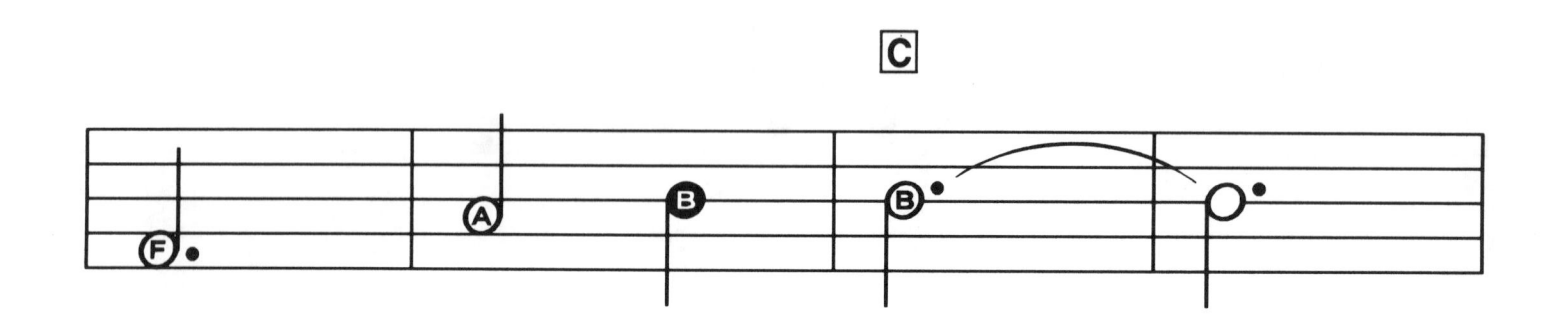

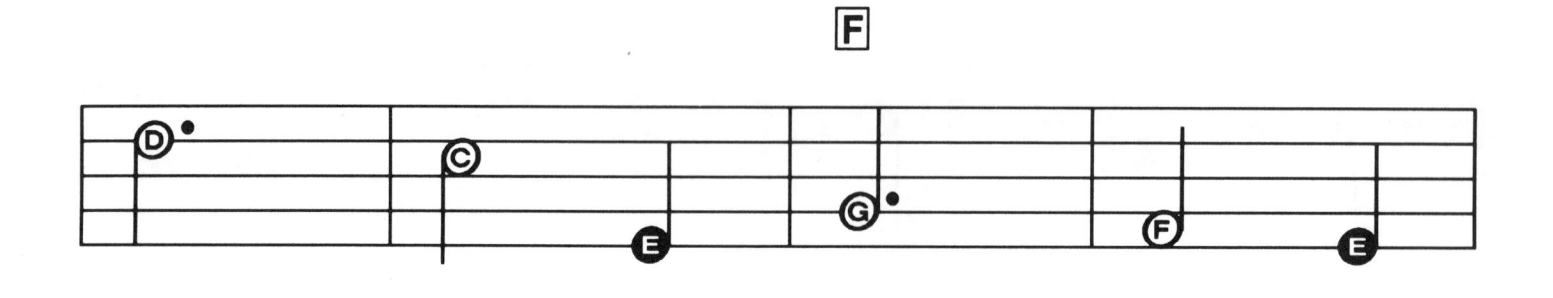

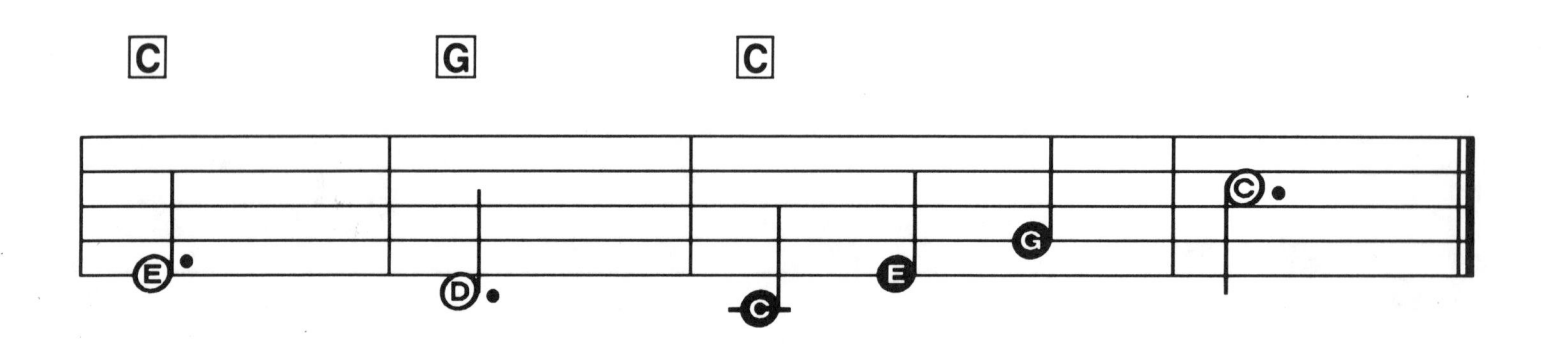

42

Copyright © 1972 HAL LEONARD CORPORATION
International Copyright Secured   All Rights Reserved

THE MAN ON THE FLYING TRAPEZE

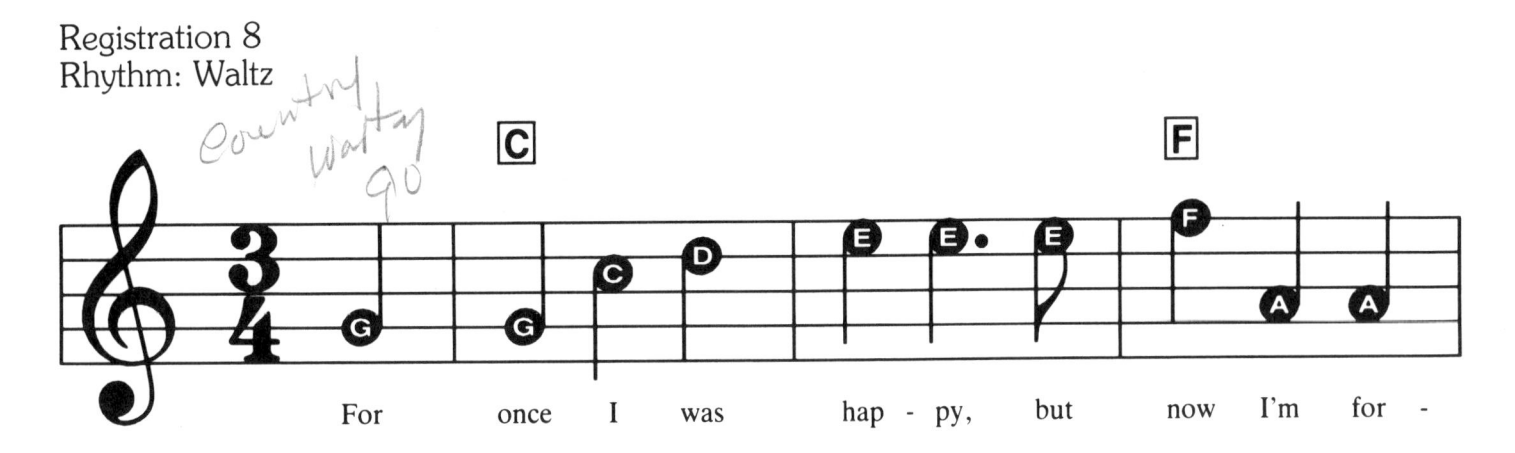

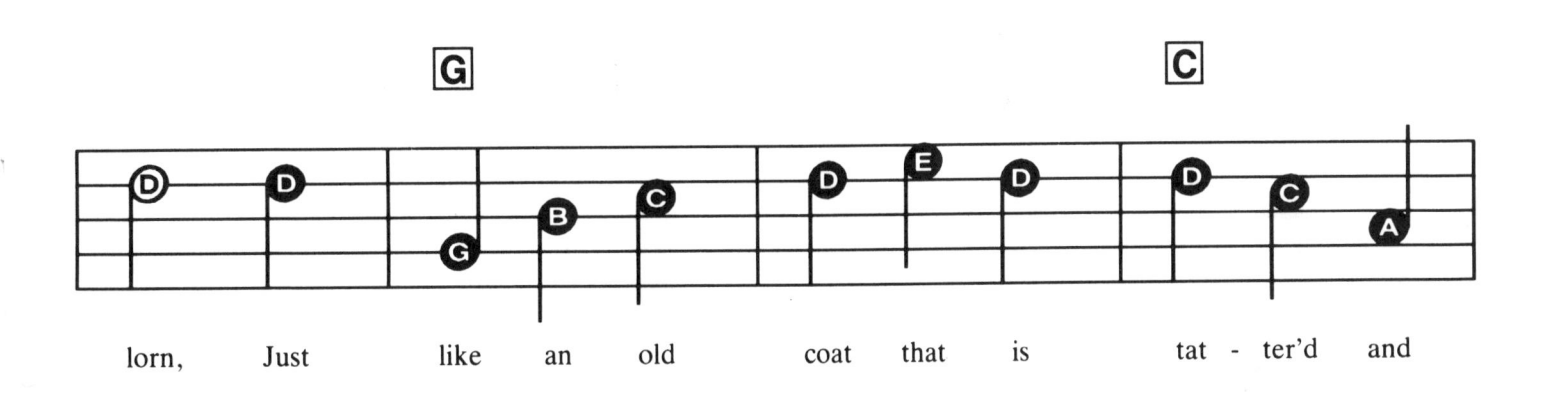

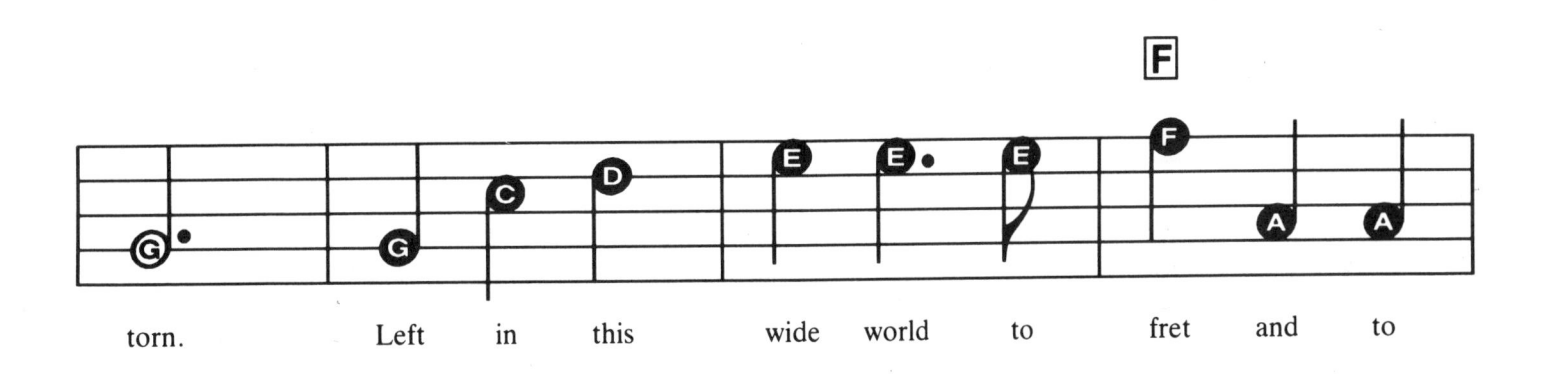

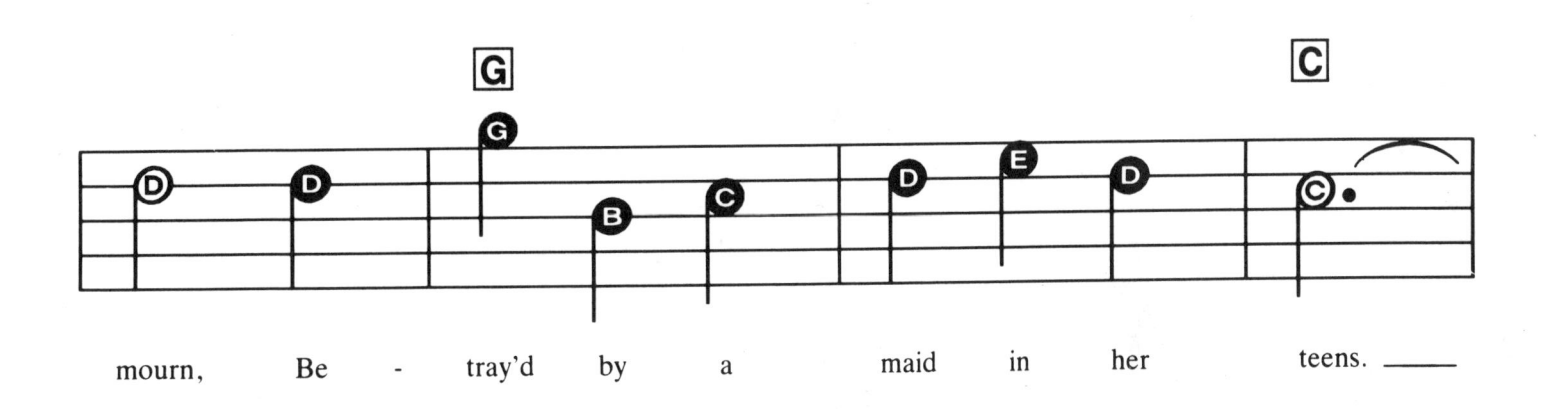

Registration 8
Rhythm: Waltz

For once I was hap - py, but now I'm for - lorn, Just like an old coat that is tat - ter'd and torn. Left in this wide world to fret and to mourn, Be - tray'd by a maid in her teens.

Copyright © 1972 HAL LEONARD CORPORATION
International Copyright Secured   All Rights Reserved

Now this girl that I loved, she was hand-some,

And I tried all I knew, her to please,

But I never could please her one quar-ter so well As the man on the

44

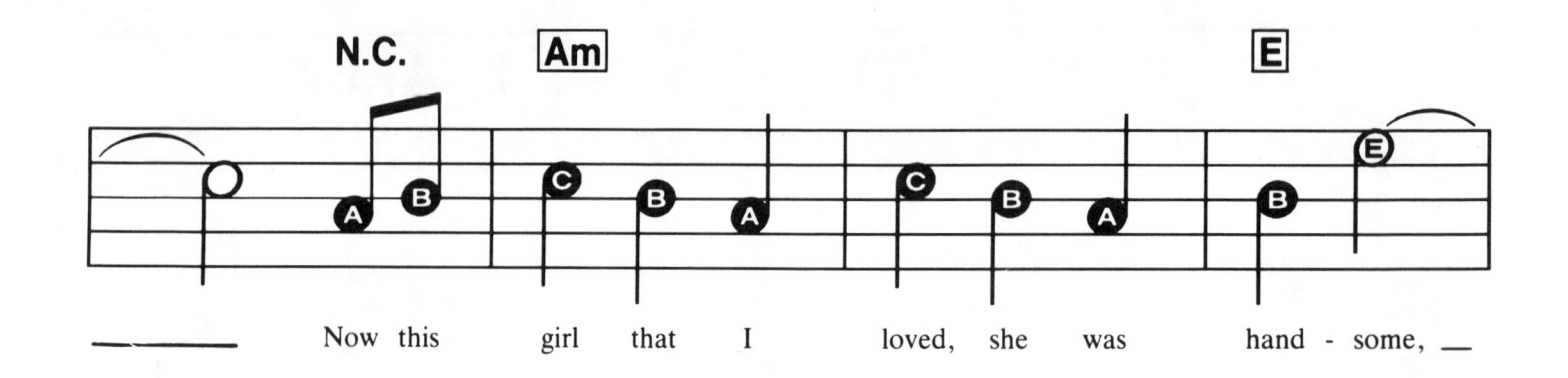

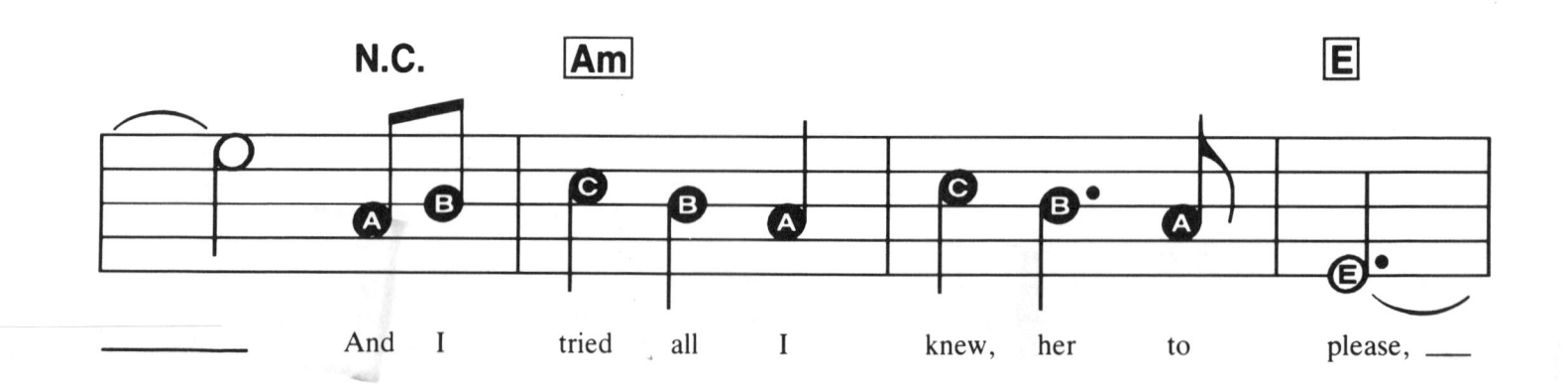

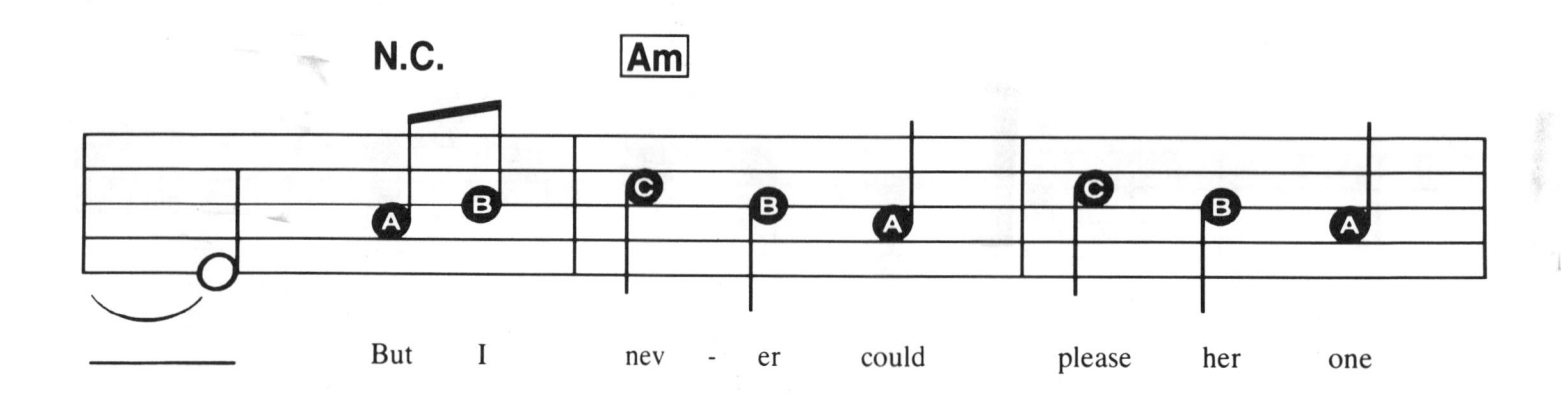

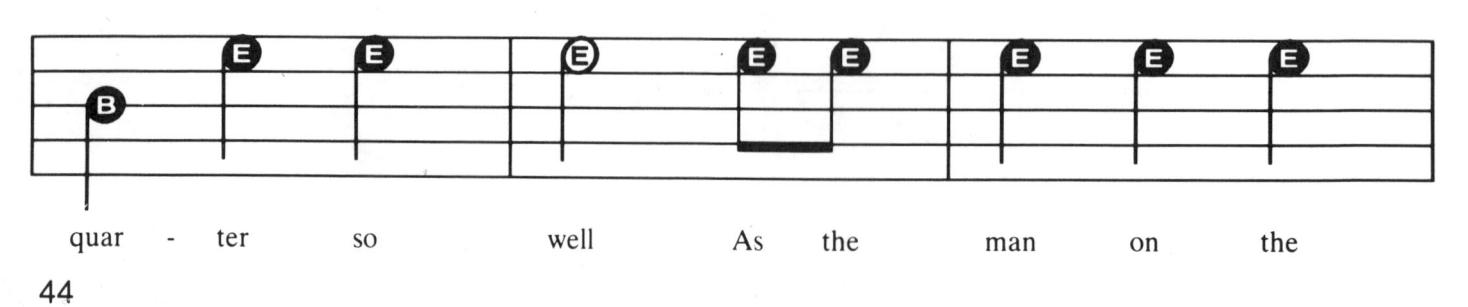

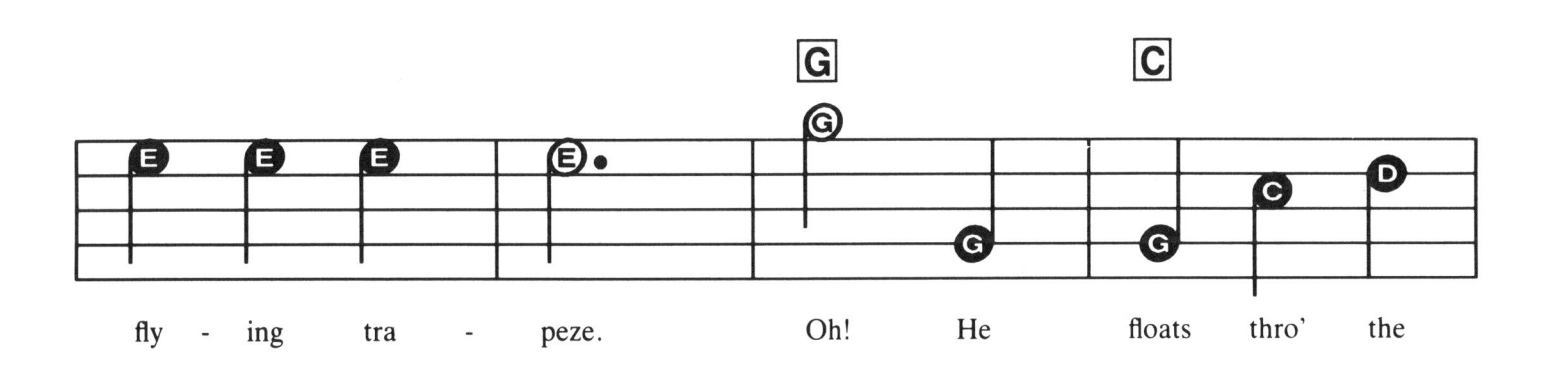

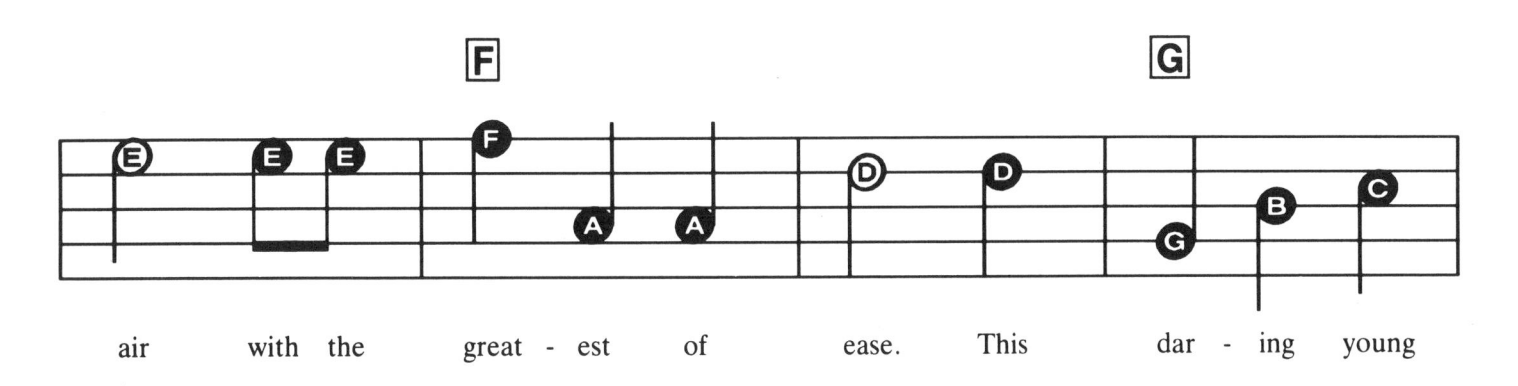

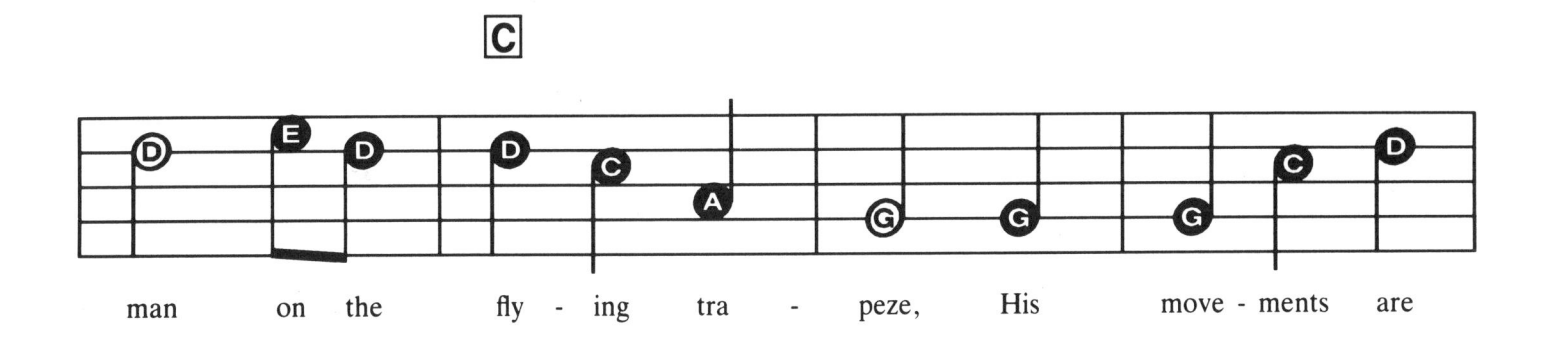

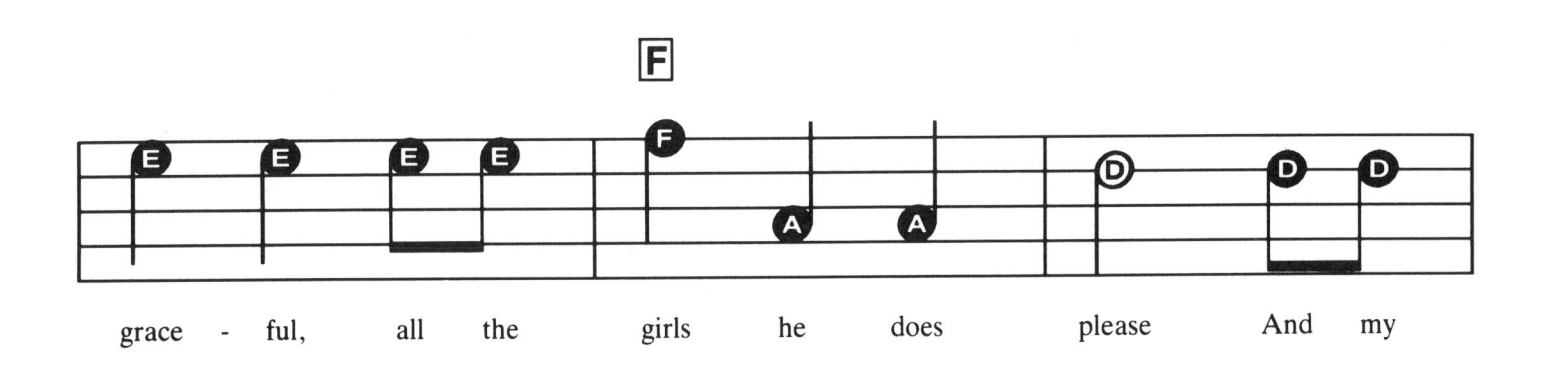

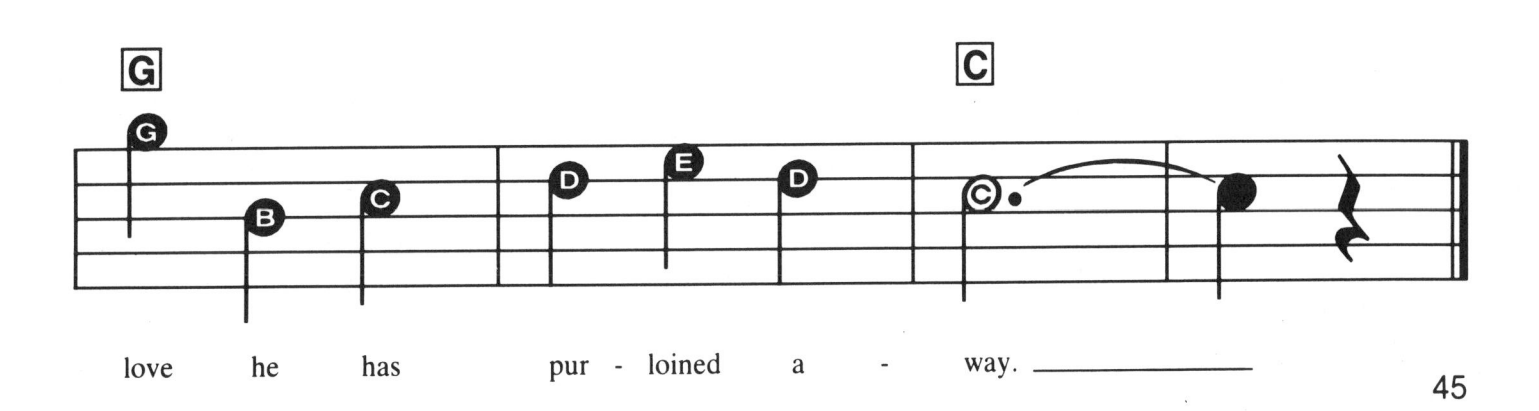

fly - ing tra - peze. Oh! He floats thro' the air with the great - est of ease. This dar - ing young man on the fly - ing tra - peze, His move - ments are grace - ful, all the girls he does please And my love he has pur - loined a - way. _____

45

MARIANNE

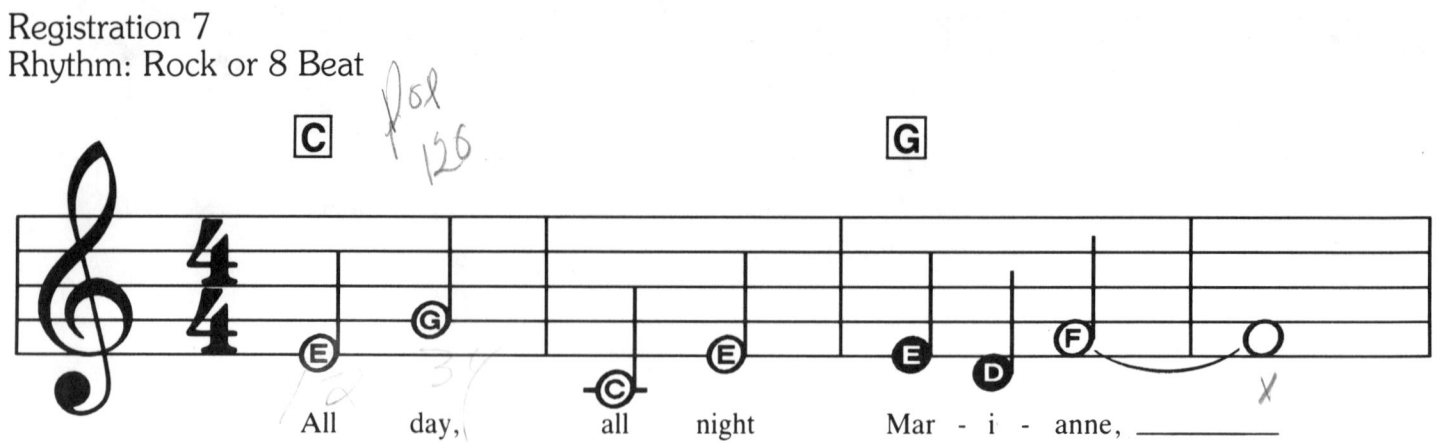

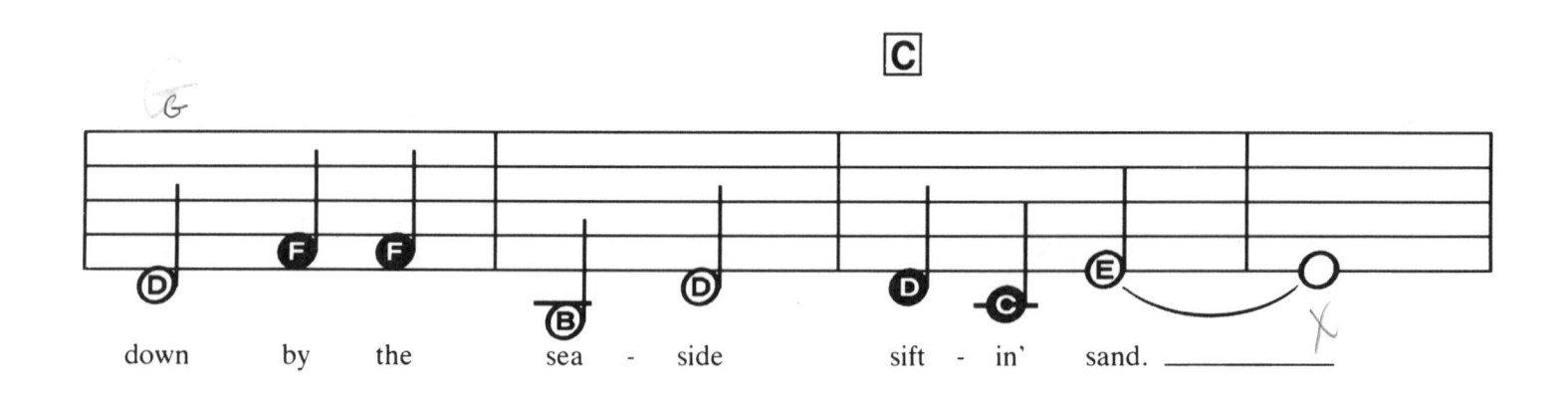

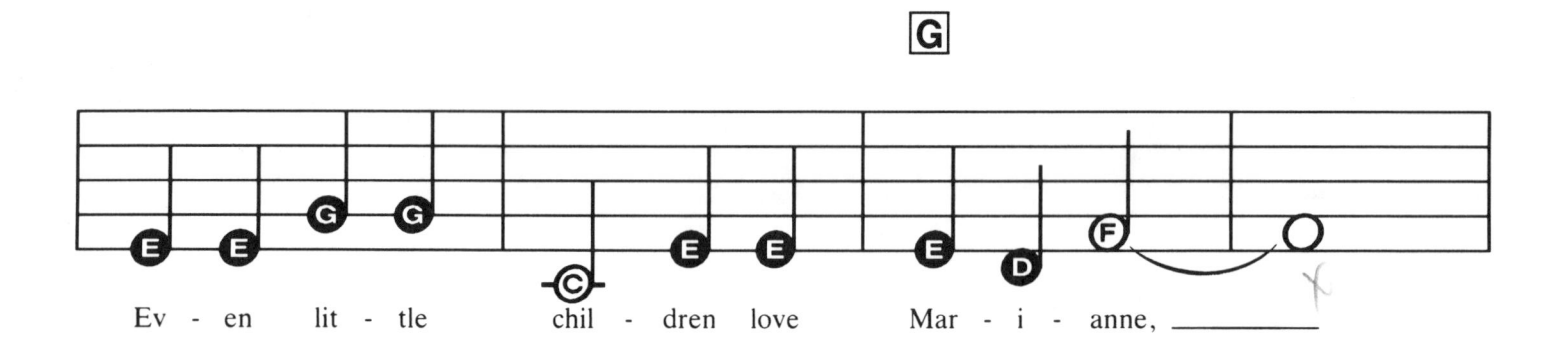

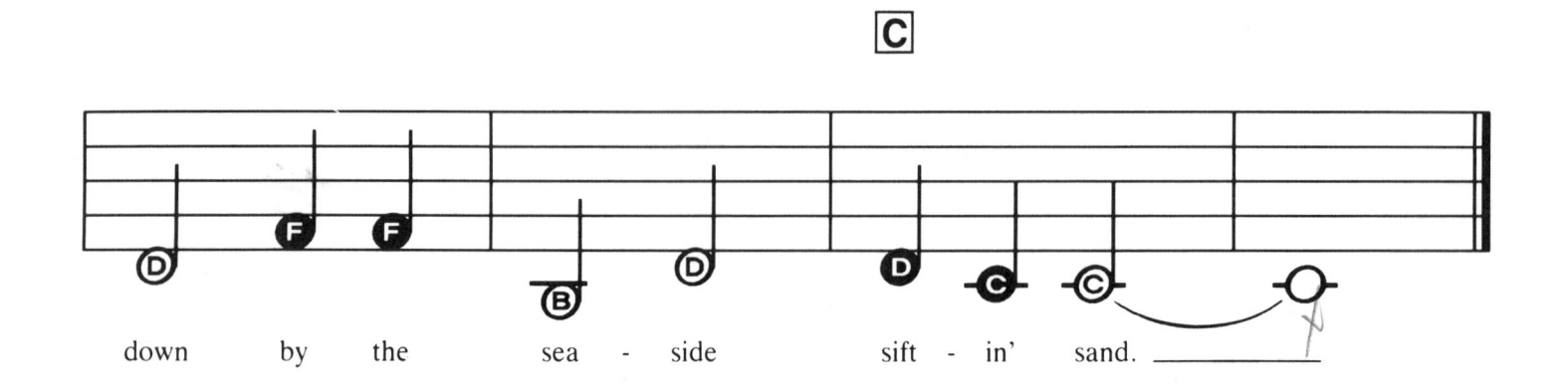

Registration 7
Rhythm: Rock or 8 Beat

[C] E G | [G] C E | E D F ~ | ~ |
All day, all night Mar-i-anne,

[G] D F F | B D | [C] D C E ~ | ~ |
down by the sea-side sift-in' sand.

[G] E E G G | C E E | E D F ~ | ~ |
Ev-en lit-tle chil-dren love Mar-i-anne,

[C] D F F | B D | D C C ~ | ~ |
down by the sea-side sift-in' sand.

46

Copyright © 1972 HAL LEONARD CORPORATION
International Copyright Secured All Rights Reserved

E-Z Play Today Registration Guide

- Match the Registration number on the song to the corresponding numbered category below. Select and activate an instrumental sound available on your instrument.
- Choose an automatic rhythm appropriate to the mood and style of the song. (Consult your Owner's Guide for proper operation of automatic rhythm features.)
- Adjust the tempo and volume controls to comfortable settings.

Registration

1	Flute, Pan Flute, Jazz Flute
2	Clarinet, Organ
3	Violin, Strings
4	Brass, Trumpet, Bass
5	Synth Ensemble, Accordion, Brass
6	Pipe Organ, Harpsichord
7	Jazz Organ, Vibraphone, Vibes, Electric Piano, Jazz Guitar
8	Piano, Electric Piano
9	Trumpet, Trombone, Clarinet, Saxophone, Oboe
10	Violin, Cello, Strings